THE BUSINESSMAN AND THE CITY

THE BUSINESSMAN AND THE CITY

THE BUSINESSMAN AND THE CITY

David L. Birch
Assistant Professor of Business Administration
Harvard University

An Analysis of the Business and Urban Affairs
Conference, Sponsored by the Harvard
Business School Association
Washington, D.C., May 1966

Harvard University
Graduate School of Business Administration
Boston . 1967

Foreword

The Harvard Business School Association is an organization composed of approximately 30,000 alumni of the Harvard Graduate School of Business Administration. While many of its members are active in constructive work aimed toward solving various urban problems in the cities in which they live, it has become increasingly apparent to the leaders of our alumni activities that there remains a large, untapped source of energy and competence in this group. In our travels around the country visiting various local HBS clubs, the most frequent comment we hear is that our alumni would like to do something to make the world a better place. Many of them feel they are getting substantial job satisfaction but want to do something productive which is totally unrelated to the advancement of their own careers.

The Washington gathering on which this book is based represents an attempt by the leaders of the Harvard Business School Association to bring together businessmen, Harvard Business School Faculty, and government officials, and to ask them to reach an understanding, first as to what can be done to solve our urban problems, second as to the role of business and its interplay with our federal government in attacking these problems, and third as to what the individual businessman attending the conference might do of a productive nature in his own city.

No meeting of this kind completely accomplishes its objectives. It is all too easy to be inspired at the moment only to return home and become wrapped up once again in familiar, day-to-day problems. On the other hand, we are beginning to see an increasing number of business executives who are taking specific action steps in attempts to improve their cities. We can only hope that in some small way this May 20, 1966, Washington gathering contributed to a better understanding between business and government as to what the businessman might do to help.

I would be most remiss if I did not express deep gratitude to both George P. Baker, Dean of the Harvard Business School, for unstinting devotion of his personal time and that of many of the key people of the School, particularly Paul W. Cherington, James J. Hill Professor of Transportation, and to John W. Macy, Chairman of the Civil Service Commission, for his untiring efforts on the government side. The fact that these highly esteemed gentlemen sponsored this program was responsible for any success that it might have had.

RALPH F. LEWIS
President, Harvard Business School Association,
1965-1966

New York
October 1967

Preface

As you read on, it will become quite clear that this book is based upon the work of many people. It is their complete cooperation which has made the book possible.

Before mentioning the special contributions of certain individuals, I would like to express my gratitude to a number of groups. First is the group of participants listed at the end of the book. They read background papers, they came long distances, and they struggled mightily with some very tough issues. Second is the group of participants whom I have quoted—particularly the keynote speakers. Each speaker has painstakingly gone over a transcript of his remarks, and each one has released the transcript for publication without major revision. The reader is thus left with a remarkably uncensored account of what happened on May 20, 1966. Finally, I would like to thank all those members of the Harvard Business School Faculty who assisted me in the preparation of the background papers. Of particular assistance were Professor Thomas C. Raymond and Assistant Professor Lewis M. Schneider.

No conference just happens. It is conceived, and it is organized. In this instance, three men late in 1965 had the imagination and the foresight to realize that, if the cities of this country were to remain inhabitable, businessmen would have to play a part, and that it was time to start doing something about it. These three men were Ralph F. Lewis, at that time President of the Harvard Business School Alumni Association, John W. Macy, Jr., Chairman of the Civil Service Commission, and Charles D. Orth, Assistant Dean and Director of Alumni Programs at the Harvard Business School. Under the leadership of Ralph Lewis, and with the support and encouragement of Dean George P. Baker, they worked out the multitude of conceptual and administrative details that go into the making of an effective, smoothly run program.

From the start, there has been one person who has been concerned with the content of both the conference and this book. He has read and commented on the various drafts leading up to this final version. He has offered encouragement many times when the manuscript might otherwise have been abandoned, and, perhaps most importantly, he has held up a high standard whenever the pressures of time have led to inaccuracies or omissions. I am most grateful to Professor Paul W. Cherington.

As in any publication, there are the all-important people who see that a manuscript is transformed from yellow paper and pencil into printed form. It has been typed by many. Of particular help were Mrs. Mary Swanson and Miss Suzanne Strauss. Miss Hilma Holton has cheerfully struggled with the problem of putting the final draft into printed form.

Finally, I would like to thank my wife, Louisa, for reading and commenting so thoughtfully on the background papers and chapters as they have progressed.

None of those mentioned above agree with everything I have said. It should thus be made very clear in closing that any conclusions which have been drawn or any inferences which have been made are my own.

DAVID L. BIRCH

Soldiers Field
Boston, Massachusetts
October 1967

Table of Contents

THE BUSINESSMAN AND THE CITY

THE BUSINESSMAN AND THE CITY

CHAPTER I

Introduction

On May 20, 1966 a small group of businessmen and government officials gathered in Washington to discuss urban problems. It was a high-level group drawn together by the Harvard Business School Association, the Business School Faculty, and The White House.[1] The purpose of the gathering was to discuss the businessman's role in solving the serious problems of America's urban areas —the areas where most business is conducted and the areas where businessmen are frequently called upon for leadership. The focus was clearly on action and how it could be most effectively taken.

The purpose of this monograph is to convey, in somewhat condensed form, what took place at the conference. Originally it was feared that, by the time the monograph would be ready for publication, it would be out-of-date. This is hardly the case. In fact, the recent passage of the Demonstration Cities and Metropolitan Development Act of 1966, the Clean Rivers Restoration Act of 1966, and the Urban Mass Transportation Act of 1966 heightens rather than diminishes the significance of the conference. Many of the government officials who attended were working on these bills, and their views on the significance of the bills are of great current interest and will remain so for some time to come.

Structure of the Conference

The number of participants was purposely limited to 100 to facilitate active participation on the part of everyone present. The structure of the conference reflected this same objective.

The program began with three keynote addresses, each followed by an active question and answer period. Next came lunch and

---

[1] See the list of participants on page 215.

President Johnson's address, read by John Macy, Chairman of the Civil Service Commission, due to a last minute shift in the President's schedule. The afternoon was devoted to five concurrent discussion groups, each of which addressed itself to a particular topic. The five topics were: housing and urban renewal, urban transportation, education, air and water pollution, and social problems.

The conference ended with a joint session in which each discussion leader summarized his group's accomplishments.

Structure of the Monograph

The monograph begins with the three keynote addresses by Robert C. Weaver, Secretary of Housing and Urban Development; Jerome P. Cavanagh, Mayor of Detroit; and John T. Ryan, President of Mine Safety Appliances Company. Following these is the President's address.

The bulk of the monograph is devoted to an analysis of the five afternoon seminars. The chapters covering each seminar include the background papers distributed to the participants in advance and any journal introductory remarks in addition to selected excerpts from an edited transcript of the seminar proceedings. It should be made clear at the outset that quotations have not been taken in the order in which they were made, and that, in the interest of continuity and brevity, much of the overall transcript has been omitted.

Following each of the seminar chapters is a selected bibliography, should the reader wish to pursue further the issues raised in the chapter.

The Challenge

The central question in the minds of those who worked on the conference was the extent to which the participants would come to grips with the problems of action. Conferences are not known for their focus on action. Yet, each participant was chosen specifically because he was in a position to take action. Would it be possible, in one day, to cut through the myriad of complicated, sometimes fuzzy issues and get to the question: How can we do something?

What is intriguing in retrospect is the extent to which the ability to cut through the issues varied with the subject matter. But before we can consider the results of the discussion groups, it is necessary to appreciate how the stage was set. This was the job of the keynote speakers, and this is where the monograph begins.

CHAPTER II

Three Keynote Addresses

The morning session consisted primarily of three addresses, each followed by a series of questions and answers. The question and answer periods will be included in this chapter because it is felt that they serve as important supplements to the prepared talks. The first address was that of Robert C. Weaver, Secretary of the Department of Housing and Urban Development.

Remarks by Robert C. Weaver

Secretary of the Department of Housing and Urban Development

It is a great honor for me to keynote this auspicious occasion. I have frequently said that we could really develop some high-powered solutions to our urban problems if only we could get those fellows at the Business School to get more interested. Now here we are, and I am looking forward to results commensurate with the sort of intellectual power massed in this room.

There is no escaping the fact that all of us are bound together inextricably in the complex urban situation. Seven out of ten of our people live in cities and suburbs today, and more will live there in the future. They are the customers and the constituents of both business and government. For better or for worse, this nation must plan for the future in terms of an urban destiny.

Unfortunately, although we have been in the throes of an urban revolution for a hundred years, and a predominantly urban nation for at least fifty, we have had difficulty in adjusting to that reality. This was understandable in view of our political development.

Through the early years of our constitutional system, we operated under a concept of dual federalism—the conviction that Nation and State were divided by impenetrable walls of separate jurisdiction. Problems which did not fall readily to the advocates of states' rights, or to those who favored more federal centralization, were swept under the rug and forgotten.

But as the nation developed, older antagonisms became subjugated to the need for solving new problems of economic and social growth. And so a new sort of federalism evolved—a cooperative federalism. This brought together programs and activities of shared responsibility through the device of federal grants-in-aid, and resulted in a measure of collaboration on a number of fronts.

But the conviction remained that expansion of power on one level of government worked to lessen power in another. Spheres of cooperation were largely restricted to policy execution and administration—not mutual development of new activities. Thus the New Deal was essentially a national and limited response to an emergency, not a fundamental change in the processes of government.

Nevertheless, the federal involvement in housing and in the cities has increased steadily in the last three decades. Millions of decent homes were built with the support of federal mortgage insurance in FHA and Veterans Administration programs. The Public Housing Program was the first meaningful attack on the slums and it was later joined by the Urban Renewal Program. But these programs were piecemeal and often administered without sufficient attention to the impact they would have on other programs, on the urban environment, or on the people involved in them.

This was true on a number of federal programs. So we had these situations:

- Public housing was initially represented primarily as a public works, with incidental reference to its social aspects. Inevitably, inadequate attention was paid to the most pressing problems of its most disadvantaged tenants.
- Urban renewal focused on clearance and downtown renewal, often without sufficient consideration for its effect on adjoining neighborhoods and the displaced.
- The highway program was designed to span America, but it changed almost absent-mindedly the development pattern and transportation network of every metropolitan area.

• The federally insured mortgage programs filled the suburbs with new homes, but often without the rational and economic planning of basic facilities or with little concern for the central cities. This led to urban sprawl in the suburbs and accelerated urban decay in core areas.

But we learned as we went along, and in the sixties we came to realize the need for a systematic approach to deal with the complex system that embraced city and suburb and entire metropolitan areas. As the magnitude of separate urban aid programs—and their interrelations and contradictions—came home to us, we began a major reexamination of existing policy. We refined and expanded the good existing programs and brought in new programs more suited to our times and more sensitive to the rapidly changing pressures and powers in an increasingly pluralistic society.

In rapid succession came provisions for open space land, for the redirection of some mortgage credit programs to support the needs of special urban populations, the beginnings of reconciliation between renewal and highway planning, and assistance to mass transportation systems. We turned from an emphasis on clearance in the urban renewal program and paid more attention to rehabilitation and code enforcement.

There came as well general recognition of these facts:

• The spread city, encompassing core city, suburbs, and fringe, was here to stay. The real issue was not to bemoan its existence, but to find ways to make it function better.

• Since the form of urban development was relatively fixed, the critical issue became one of improving the quality of life for those in the city—extending the options of its citizens, and alleviating the conditions that led to discrimination, neighborhood disintegration and the alienation of the individual.

It is a distressing fact that the humanizing influence of the city has deteriorated seriously in recent years. The city has traditionally provided a way station for the waves of immigrants who came from abroad. There were hardships, but there was also the opportunity to learn the language and new skills and to move up the long tenement trail to relative affluence and acceptance into American society. But the most recent urban immigrant labored under special difficulties—he was old, or handicapped, or he was nonwhite. In some city neighborhoods, blight and poverty have gone hand-in-hand for generations, and the slum is no longer a way station. The bus has stopped running to the suburbs and the urban poor are increasingly insulated from the larger society.

But events of 1964 and 1965 contributed to meeting these problems. Consider this sampling:

- With the Economic Opportunity program, the Administration launched the first concerted attack directed not only at alleviating the distress of the impoverished, but at attacking the root-causes of poverty.
- President Johnson became the first President in history to make the general conditions of urban life a separate matter of official concern—in his message on the central city and its suburbs in 1965.
- For the first time in a generation, the Congress authorized a genuinely new program to increase the inventory of low-income housing—the rent supplement plan.
- For the first time in history, the President and the Congress concurred in the creation of a federal department—Housing and Urban Development—to meet the needs of the urban citizen.
- In an historic speech at Ann Arbor, Michigan, the President introduced the concept of Creative Federalism, which takes over from the earlier problem-solving techniques and has become a guidepost for the future.

I understand the President may speak to you at lunch, and if so it may be that he will enlarge on this concept. So I will restrict my remarks to the effect of Creative Federalism on the new urban programs and proposals which come under my Department.

I mentioned earlier the dual federalism of our early history, and the cooperative federalism that came later. Creative Federalism leads us to the next long step forward. The President defined this new federalism as embodying "new concepts of cooperation between the National Capital and the leaders of local communities." As we have seen subsequently, he meant private as well as public leadership.

Unlike earlier brands, Creative Federalism does not conceive of power as a static commodity, to be transferred from private to public sectors or state to national levels at the expense of the earlier possessor of power. Public policy, rather, arises in response to new needs and conditions and changes as pressures change. And the energies of the creative response from all levels and sectors in turn galvanize the federal sector into positive action.

Today, concern over issues has given way to concern for broad problems. As contemporary problems such as poverty, social disorganization, civil rights and rampant urbanization become readily identified, Creative Federalism responds with solutions instead of ideologies.

In the broad framework, it stresses local initiative and local solutions to local problems. The federal role continues to be one of support for locally initiated and locally administered activities. But this is not a passive role. Where the obvious needs for action to meet an urban problem are not being fulfilled, the federal government has a responsibility at least to generate a thorough awareness of the problem.

With this concept to guide us, we are now ready to orchestrate all our programs and to bring together efforts of all levels of the government and the private sector to develop solutions for the full range of urban problems.

To meet this goal, President Johnson called for a decade of experimentation. And in January of this year, he instituted that decade with a new set of federal urban programs.

One of these is the Urban Development Act—one of the most significant federal proposals for better planning in the nation's history. Under it, the federal government will provide real dollar incentives for better metropolitan planning, while at the same time putting a premium upon the most economic and orderly development of those physical improvements which reinforce planning itself.

These incentives come in the form of supplemental payments for those existing programs which have an effect on the overall development of metropolitan areas. These include such activities as sewer and water, sewage treatment plants, construction of primary and secondary roads, urban mass transportation, open space acquisition and public works and facilities.

Supplemental grants would be up to 20% of the cost of any project, up to a maximum of 80% of federal funding. The emphasis is on planned development. This program realizes there is no simple or final solution to urban sprawl. It exists. It will not go away. It realizes that the federal government cannot advocate or condone federal planning controls. But it does offer federal incentives and financial support which can activate metropolitan organizations and compacts to give the direction to metropolitan growth.

In this Act, we have also asked for funds for a series of Urban Information Centers. These centers will not only develop new information on urban problems, but will also coordinate and disseminate much of the information which is now in existence but scattered in varied forms, with limited usefulness. Grants for such centers would be made to states and metropolitan area-wide agencies.

The third proposal in this Act is that which is intended to help shape whole areas into economic and delightful new communities. Last year, the Congress passed a program of mortgage insurance, under FHA, for land development. Nearly seventy proposals have been received under this program, and the first commitment has already been made.

Now we have asked the Congress for expansion of this program, to permit loans of up to $25 million rather than the $10 million initially set. This would permit developers to put forth greater effort to build whole new communities, with a full range of needed community facilities.

We have also asked for an additional $95 million for mass transportation, with some $10 million of this for demonstrations of new or improved techniques. This is an essential expansion of a good existing program.

The other major new proposal is more inner-directed—to the heart of the city. It is the ultimate response, as of now, to the concept of Creative Federalism as it relates to the city.

The Demonstration Cities Program is the first major effort to cope coherently with the whole complex of urban problems. Its aim is the total improvement in the lives of the affected community population, and a basic change in the whole community.

The Demonstration Cities Program, now before Congress, works like this: The city itself selects a target area within its boundaries, according to the following criteria:

(1) The area must be large enough to remove blighted conditions throughout whole sections or neighborhoods;

(2) The target area should be largely residential, containing a substantial share of a city's substandard housing;

(3) The program must be designed to upgrade the living environment for poor and disadvantaged families and individuals.

The success of the program depends entirely on local initiative. The city must be willing and able to use local public and private resources. It must be willing to undertake actions that will have widespread effects on the physical and social structure of the city. And the federal government will commit its total resources to support these actions.

In addition to regular federal program funds, special federal grants equal to 80% of the local share of the federal programs involved, would be extended to Demonstration areas. These grants would supplement normal grant-in-aid funds, to be used for any purpose within the framework of the development plan.

Under the program, new and rehabilitated housing would be created, at rents or prices geared to the incomes of the people in the area. Most of this would be provided through improvement of existing housing, using rehabilitation loans and grants where needed.

Schools, hospitals, neighborhood facilities for community health, and recreational centers, parks and open spaces, would be part of the plan. Public facilities—sewers, water, streets and mass transportation—and public services, such as better police and fire protection, could also be included.

These activities deal largely with major physical facilities and services. Equally as basic, however, would be the programs for social and human betterment, designed to raise aspirations and help provide the skills and motivation to realize those aspirations.

Today these programs for rebuilding lives have been greatly expanded to include a wide range of federal grants-in-aid, covering manpower training, vocational education and rehabilitation, employment assistance, special education for deprived children, and the anti-poverty community action programs.

The President asked for some $2.3 billion to fund this vital Demonstration Cities Program. For the first year, an additional $12 million would be needed to develop plans and programs. Following that, an average of about $400 million a year would be needed for the redevelopment of demonstration urban areas on the scale which is needed if cities are to be recaptured from the clutch of blight and social disorganization. But in the process, the Demonstration Cities Program will not reduce the amount of federal grants-in-aid that would go to other cities in the absence of the new program.

This is an experimental and innovative program, and the essence of the breed is that there should be a period of testing and adjustment. Once the demonstrations prove effective, we can apply and reapply them in cities throughout the land.

We must also keep in mind the strain on our budget and the realistic allocation of our natural resources to meet all our responsibilities—at home and abroad—when we consider the level of expenditure involved.

The President called eloquent attention to our obligations as a great democracy in his speech of May 11 at Princeton University.

The issue of this generation, he said, "has to do with the obligations of power in the world for a society that strives, despite its worst flaws, to be just and humane."

He said: "Surely it is not a paranoid vision of America's place in the world to recognize that freedom is still indivisible—still has adversaries whose challenge must be answered."

And he outlined a credo: "The aims for which we struggle are aims which, in the ordinary course of affairs, men of the intellectual world applaud and serve: the principle of choice over coercion, the defense of the weak against the strong and aggressive, the right of a young and frail nation to develop free from the interference of her neighbors. . . ."

We can fulfill this obligation as well as those to our own people, and we have been doing so. And with the cooperation of the private sector and by exercising prudence and good sense in our national outlays, we can take the next step forward: the revitalization of our cities and the rehabilitation of our deprived citizens. We can get on with what the President has asked us to do in 1966, to bring about "a year of rebirth for American cities."

DISCUSSION FOLLOWING SECRETARY WEAVER'S REMARKS

QUESTION: I wonder if Secretary Weaver would care to comment on the reluctance of local politicians to allow some of these things to be promoted by the business citizens because of the disrupting effect it has on the constituents.

MR. WEAVER: I think the next speaker, the eminent Mayor of Detroit, would be in a better position to comment on that than I would. My guess would be that this is probably a two-way street, and that probably the great requirement here is first to be able to get some sort of conversation and discussion going on between the business community and the local government. I have noticed that Mayor Lindsay has been having some slight difficulty in this department. It seems as though he made the overture, but the response was not too great on the other side. I am only suggesting that this is probably a problem that has something to be said on both sides, and, since I am in the middle, I will keep quiet on it.

QUESTION: I am not sure whether I am correctly informed, but on the Demonstration Cities Program, I understand that Mr. Cavanagh and Mr. Lindsay have reaped all the money for themselves. Is there to be money spread around for smaller areas for different demonstrations?

MR. WEAVER: Yes. It will go into cities and towns, both large and small. I think that a demonstration program is not a program of total solution. If we had all of the knowledge, and if we had all of the answers to all of these problems, we wouldn't need the demonstration. The Mayor [of Detroit] is here and will speak for himself—without any hesitancy I am sure.

I think that there is no question—knowing New York City better than I know Detroit—that New York City could absorb two billion dollars, and up to two and a half billion dollars, of federal funds over five or six years and still not solve its urban problem. We are not trying, in the Model Cities Demonstration Program, to solve the total urban problem. We are trying in the demonstration project to select sizable areas and to solve their total problems, in a series of cities under a series of different circumstances, so as to get a series of new techniques and of new knowledge. We are trying out the hypotheses that we have; we are trying out the coordination that seems to be inevitable.

So we will have not a pattern, but a series of patterns which will be available to us at that time when, because of budgetary situations and because of other circumstances, we will be able to put the type of money in Detroit or in New York that the two mayors would like to have put in there and get the maximum result from it. We will have a pattern of successes and failures, because some of these things aren't going to work the way we assume they're going to work.

Let me say this—and here I sometimes differ with some of my friends who are the mayors—I think if I were a mayor, and if I were a city councilman also, that I would feel as they do: the pressing problem and certainly the most immediate problem that the cities face is a problem of money. Without more money, our cities are not going to survive. The only way I can see them getting it is from the states or federal government. I don't see it coming in large volume from the states, so it has got to be from the federal government. There is no question about that, in my opinion.

On the other hand, I think with all the money that might be needed, there has also got to be more know-how. There has got to be more experimentation. There have got to be more attempts at doing things. This is what the Model Cities Program is trying to do. Not to solve the national urban problem, but to create a series of experiments and a series of demonstrations, first, to prove that it can be done, and secondly, to discover how it can be done most effectively and most efficiently.

QUESTION: I was wondering, in view of that statement, Mr. Secretary, and in view of the apparent mood of the Congress with respect to urban transit—apparently they are willing to give you almost twice as much as you asked for—why didn't you ask for more?

MR. WEAVER: For the Model Cities Demonstration Program? I
think for two reasons. In the first place, there is such a thing as a
budget, you know. This happens to be a period of great strain,
with our foreign commitments and with Vietnam. Secondly, if
we are going to have a demonstration, we have to have some idea
of the number of cities that are going to participate. We don't
know which cities will participate. We do know the general
capabilities of cities, and with the high criteria that have been
established—and this is a quality program—we believe that most
of the cities which would be able to do the type of job that is required under this program could be funded under it. We could
have doubled the size of it, and instead of having what we are
thinking about now in a large city—a program involving some
35,000 families, which means about 100,000 people—we could
have gone, in a large city, maybe to 70,000 families and 200,000
people. What we tried to do was to get the most reasonable size,
from the point of view of the budget and the possibility of getting
through the Congress, which would make possible a sizable
demonstration. This is a matter of judgment. Others may feel
otherwise; the Congress may feel otherwise. They may increase
it; they may decrease it. This we don't know, if they act favorably
upon it at all. There is no magic about our figures except we
think that they are feasible and we think that this is a reasonable
size of demonstration both from the point of view of its objective
and, secondly, from the point of view of being able to find a sufficient number of takers willing, able, and ready to go ahead and
do the type of job that the program envisions. This is a subjective
evaluation. Somebody else could come up with a different set of
figures, and they will just have to argue about it. It is subjective,
not objective.

QUESTION: Mr. Secretary, what are some of the major hypotheses
that you are trying to demonstrate in some of these early programs?

MR. WEAVER: The first hypothesis is that it is possible, by combining physical, financial, social, and human considerations and
programs, and by coordinating these programs in a total attack
on deprived and depressed areas, to be able to rehabilitate the
areas both physically and humanly. By bringing in all of the tools
that we now have and supplementing them by a few other things
that could be either peripheral or novel, that we can make a

major impact on these areas and we can revitalize them. This is the basic concept.

Secondly, that if we take all of the existing programs and maximize them by putting them on a target area and by coordinating them, the net result is going to be more than just adding them up as individual uncoordinated entities. This is so obvious that I don't think it needs any delineation.

The third major hypothesis is that, by attempting this type of program, we will accomplish several things which are peripheral to the particular activity in itself. For example, we will be able to get many more coordinated programs of the type that a few of our cities now have. We have a few cities which have coordinated these programs and the results have been quite outstanding. This will encourage that type of activity elsewhere without having a federal fiat saying that you have to do it in a particular way.

Also, we believe that if we are able to do this, we are going to be able to take the two billion, three, four, five, six or seven hundred million dollars, and attract a tremendous lot of private funds as well. For example, one of the ways the rehabilitation will be carried on will be by a temporary acquisition—or acquisition by a public body—of houses, having them brought up to a certain standard, and then selling them back into the private market. We will get a flow of private money constantly coming back and releasing our public funds. Also, we would use the write-down, which is possible under urban renewal, in connection with rehabilitation, so that these houses would come back on the market at a price that matches the income of the people who are now living in the area.

We also believe it of basic importance, if minor misunderstandings are not to grow into major obstacles, to have citizen involvement. We know that this matter of citizen participation is one which has got to be spelled out much more carefully than it has been in the past if it's going to work. But it's got to happen. We have also got to work with and on our labor unions to get their cooperation because we want the people in these areas to participate as much as possible as workers to rebuild the communities in which they are going to live.

We will be concerned with breakthroughs in technology. In this morning's *Wall Street Journal*, for example, there is an article—a lead article—on our experimentation with rehabilitation.

These are technological matters, for the most part, but they are terribly important. In order to do the things which you will read about in that newspaper, we've had to negotiate with the city of New York—because the major current experiments happen to be in New York City—with the unions, with the building inspectors, and with the building department in order to be able to use some of these new approaches.

These are the types of things that we want to do. We think we are saying that if it gets the type of enthusiasm and support (and this is where you come in as a part of the local community), and it is something that the community really believes is a part of it, and something that it is dedicated to, we will be able to make certain modifications in some of these very strict straitjackets which limit the things we can do today. I am not a Pollyanna. I don't believe we are going to be able to change the whole thing. But I think we can make some significant modifications under demonstrations of this sort.

This is the beauty of it. We may be able to make a breakthrough in Detroit that we can't make in New York, assuming that either or both of these cities were in the program. We may be able to make a breakthrough in another city that we couldn't do in still a fourth city. Once these things become possible, once they capture the imagination of the American people, once you begin to believe that you can do this in your cities, I think that it will spread.

Let me say finally, from my point of view—and this is something that dominates everything that I am concerned with; it is one of the reasons why I am concerned with new communities on the one hand and why I am concerned with model cities on the other—I think that our real, basic problem has been that we have not raised the horizon of expectation of urban America to the height that it should be raised. We are selling our people short in terms of what we could do with our present affluence and with our present technical know-how. Just consider what we could do if we raise both of those, because both are going to be raised and are being raised. If we can get people excited and get people to expect and to demand more, I think we are going to be able to get many of the bottlenecks broken down. By the same token, as this goes on we are going to have to, of course, place a greater amount of our national resources into the matter of urban development. This is inevitable and I think it will come about. It is not going to come about as quickly as Jerry Cavanagh wants it to, because he wants it yesterday. And if I were in Jerry's position, I would too.

* * *

Remarks by Jerome P. Cavanagh

Mayor of Detroit, Michigan

It is indeed appropriate that the Harvard Business School Association summon some of the nation's top business leaders to today's seminar on the complicated challenges which face our urban areas. Our cities have become the arenas in which almost every difficult problem which besets our society—race relations, poverty, air and water pollution, housing, transportation, and the myriad of others—is to be found. It is where solutions must be forged. Your presence shows that our business and industrial leaders recognize the role they can play in promoting and benefiting from the inevitable processes of change.

Change, like life, is a constant condition. Nothing stands still. The only question we have, then, is whether we will seek to master change and harness it in constructive directions or whether it is to master us. I would suggest, based on our experience in Detroit, that a coalition of government, labor, and business is an indispensable ingredient for the types of meaningful changes which can beautify our cities, renew the spirits of their residents as well as the physical environment, and create a decent and livable city.

In his extremely interesting talk, Secretary Weaver has sketched out for us why it is so necessary for the federal government to play a major role in helping our cities amass the financial and technical capability to respond to their many needs. The Housing and Urban Development Act of 1965, which Dr. Weaver administers, has been most helpful to many communities because of what it has meant, and can mean, in grants for basic sewer and water projects, neighborhood facilities, advanced land acquisition, urban beautification, and what is left of the rent supplement program for families with limited incomes.

After a long period of neglect, the federal government has recognized the seriousness of the urban condition and has committed substantial resources to aid our cities. It has been a long fight, and it is no wonder that President Johnson hailed the creation of Secretary Weaver's new department as "the single most important breakthrough in the last 40 years." Legislation, however, is not enough. Government action, important as it may be, is simply not enough. We will not be able to rebuild the physical and social fabric of our cities unless American industry helps develop the new programs and policies needed to revitalize our cities and make major investments in them.

What I am suggesting is not necessarily the course of least resistance. Nor is it necessarily the course which promises the quickest or easiest return. But in the long run, progressive business involvement in the problems of our cities—your engagement in urban affairs—will yield benefits and dividends of vast and lasting consequence. And in many cases, with the close cooperation of local government officials, there are profits to be realized by closely identifying business interest with the public interest.

In 1961, Detroit was considered a badly depressed area. City finances showed a deficit of some $34.5 million and our municipal obituary had appeared in a number of national publications. Much has changed. In the past five years we have been able—with the firm backing of business—to pump new life into the city. It took a bit of a selling job at the beginning, but soon our community's leadership began to sense their self-interest in improving their city.

As a first step, we forged a consensus at the local level on the need for cooperative efforts at change. Just last year, *Fortune* magazine reported our efforts this way:

> All the diverse elements that make up Detroit's power structure, once divided and pitted against itself, are being welded together in a remarkable synthesis. Every significant accomplishment in such major areas as race relations, urban renewal and the arts—whether initiated by a single individual or by one special interest—has become the province of a board or committee

that includes representatives of the United Auto Workers, one or more of the city's utilities, the clergy, ethnic groups, retailers, the auto companies, real estate interests, finance, the press, political groups, and any other relevant interests. Though the consensus may appear to encompass a breadth of forces unlikely to do much more than create an aura of civic virtue, in Detroit the synthesized power structure has surprising effect.[2]

This is not a tribute to any individual but to a community which has made up its mind to confront its problems and attempt their solution.

The role of businessmen as part of this consensus has been particularly encouraging, in deed as well as word. The flight of industry from Detroit has been stemmed in large part, and our city has witnessed an actual expansion of industrial growth. Urban renewal funds are being used to develop modern and efficient commercial and industrial parks. With the help of the Federal Area Redevelopment Act funds were used to help private entrepreneurs build Detroit's first new hotel since the 1920s, the Pontchartrain, which sits across from Detroit's Civic and Convention center. And while government has helped business, business has helped the entire community by providing employment and help in a number of important projects of community-wide interest.

Increasingly this Detroit model of consensus and cooperative community-wide effort is becoming the national pattern. Clearly the intent of today's meeting is a step in the right direction. It has already helped refine all of our thinking about urban problems and begun a dialogue which hopefully will lead to more affirmative joint national action.

We have also learned that there is a great deal local governments can learn from business. Few countries in the world can rival—and none can surpass—the record American private enterprise has for efficiently tackling problems and solving them. Many local communities, Detroit among them, have already begun to apply the wonders of computer technology to make their operations more efficient. Some, and here we are taking a leaf from the federal

---

[2] *Fortune*, June 1965, p. 144.

government, are instituting the Planned Programming Budget System or PPBS, as it is called, to help us weigh the costs of programs against their likely benefits. This is a far more rational way to allocate our resources and a helpful tool for decision making.

Happily, the Department of Housing and Urban Development is encouraging our cities to make more use of the practical techniques and hard-nosed methods which have been used so successfully by businessmen. In fact, the whole approach of the Johnson Administration—the concept of "Creative Federalism"—is bent on assisting local communities develop local solutions to their problems. This approach does not simply substitute federal power for local determination but helps the whole process of cooperative community action. The proposed Demonstration Cities Bill—an Act which is badly needed because of its comprehensive and massive nature—will help local communities carry out their own plans to bring about the visible changes the legislation envisions. Although the Bill is still in committee, business, labor, and community leaders in Detroit are already planning a private nonprofit corporation to assist, with some $6 million in privately generated funds, the purpose of the Act.

Businessmen should be concerned with their cities for a good reason—they are directly affected by what happens in them. A beautiful city is good for business—it attracts prosperity. A decent educational system is essential for meeting the personnel requirements of the future. Proper planning can help prevent chaos and confusion. But there are other problems in our cities which deserve your earnest attention as well. These are what are often impersonally referred to as the cities' social problems. However, racial discrimination, poverty, festering and tense ghettos are not impersonal; they affect the lives of millions directly, and will soon, if more is not done, affect us all more directly. Not only were more than 30 lives lost in the Watts riots but also $43 million in property was destroyed.

In a very thoughtful speech recently the president of the Ford Motor Company, my good friend Henry Ford II, said the entire nation faces a vast peril in the social unrest which has exploded in some cities and threatens them all. More must be done, he warned, to erase the conditions which breed anger and frustration because the order and traditions of our society are at stake. "What really counts when we measure social progress," he said, "is not the ingenuity of technology but the achievement of such things as human satisfaction and fulfillment and the growth of harmony, good will and respect among men. We can compute the gross national product but we cannot compute gross national satisfaction or good will."

It should not surprise anyone that there is no human satisfaction in living in a corroded tenement in Harlem or in perpetual unemployment in Watts. We should not wonder why Watts exploded but why so many other cities did not. The fundamental discontent which is abroad in this land—and throughout the world—has legitimate roots in unmet needs and unsolved problems. We must have the foresight and the intelligence to plan wisely today to avoid the senseless and wasteful catastrophes that are the sure by-products of inaction. This is why we can never be complacent in our national posture, nor should we be unwilling to reassess our policies so as to unleash more of our vast resources toward eliminating so much unnecessary and destructive human suffering, disease, and blocked opportunities.

The main problem with the leaders of America, James Reston wrote recently in the *New York Times,* is that they are, and I quote, "so overwhelmed by the problem of doing things that they have little time left to think about what they are doing. Operations dominate purposes. The practical men have taken over from the ideological men and this has many advantages but pragmatism may be misleading us."

There are probably few among us who do not get occasionally so wrapped up in doing things that they have little time to question their approach or study possible alternatives. Yet the future of our cities—the future of our entire society—depends on how creatively we are able to respond to the problems and challenges which confront us. It is far easier to tend to the machinery of government or business than to step back for a moment and find the vision and courage to evaluate the long-term implications of our daily decisions. Yet, painful as this process might be, the dictates of change demand that we shunt aside the old cliches of yesterday and adopt a new outlook for tomorrow. In the words of Hillel:

If not you, who?

If not now, when?

DISCUSSION FOLLOWING MR. CAVANAGH'S REMARKS

QUESTION: Mayor Cavanagh, could you tell us a little bit about how you started this corporation that you spoke of that apparently is going to avail itself of the Demonstration Act? Who started it? Did your office originate it, or did the Chamber of Commerce? Who put up the funds for the legal services to draw up its charter, the travel expenses, et cetera?

MAYOR CAVANAGH: I'll talk about the actual formation and operation of one corporation that has been in operation now for a number of years and of the formation of this new corporation. They have both been formed in somewhat the same way.

When I came into office, Detroit was one of three major cities in America that still qualified as a depressed area—with persistent and chronic unemployment. Pittsburgh and Providence, Rhode Island, I think, were the other two. Detroit, however, had not bothered to qualify for any Area Redevelopment Administration funds. The Act was very cumbersome, it was true, and very difficult. Not too many businessmen that were successful—particularly in some of the major businesses there—were necessarily interested in forming corporations so they in turn could lend money to marginal type businesses. This is very understandable.

In any event, we made it sort of a civic crusade. First, we invited all the business leaders in. Subsequently, I'll have to say that what I think really caused the creation of the Metropolitan Industrial Development Corporation was the fact that Walter Reuther contributed some $25,000 in a very public way and sort of gave a little push to the other business interests in the community. As a result there was broad participation. Also, Mr. Reuther served on the Urban Task Force this year, or last year, which recommended to the President, among other things, the Demonstration Cities concept. It was one that we had sort of a proprietary interest in because I had served on the Task Force the previous year and recommended the same thing, but the President at that time didn't feel that it was appropriate to present it to Congress.

Anyway, knowing that Demonstration Cities was going to be proposed, we started some meetings with some of the business leaders and the labor leaders, including Mr. Reuther, considering the possibility of creating a private structure which would aid the municipal effort in qualifying as a Demonstration City.

Mr. Reuther himself took on much of the job of personally contacting some of the leaders of the automobile companies. I had talked to a number of business leaders. We got some sort of agreement before we publicly unveiled it at the first meeting: that the business community and the labor community were committed to the proposition of having Detroit qualify, and that they recognized the need to create a corporation outside of the structure of government—a nonprofit corporation—which would aid government in the so-called designation as a Demonstration City.

Some seed money already has been committed by these same interests—both the business and the labor groups. They see this as an additional tool for the city and a way in which private groups can really mobilize their interests. It won't be a municipal corporation. It will be a private, nonprofit corporation that will act really as sort of a revolving fund to spur or stimulate increased development in the so-called Demonstration City Target Area. Right now we have the by-laws and the charter being drawn up—in the same fashion that we had the other corporation's by-laws and charter drawn up—by attorneys from all the major business interests and the unions. They have formed a legal committee. We have set up finance committees and subcommittees.

The interesting thing is the fact that all of the major business interests I know of in Detroit, including those that are represented here, are actively involved in it—not just some person whom they might designate. Walter Cisler, Chairman of the Board of Detroit Edison, is involved, and I am not sure whether it's Frank Colombo or Joe Hudson, the Chairman or the President, of J. L. Hudson and Company. These are the men that are actually serving. That's the only way that these things really work. If they designate some third assistant, who is in charge of governmental affairs, to sit on the boards of these corporations, they never really move because the decisions are obviously made by other people. This is why I've got a rule of thumb in Detroit that we don't go to the well too often and request the presence of men like Frank Colombo or Joe Hudson or Henry Ford or Lynn Townsend. But when we do I think they all know that it's an issue of some importance and that they generally wind up serving personally at that point.

QUESTION: Originally, your problem was employment and you formed an Industrial Development Corporation. Well, the Demonstration Cities Program is housing-oriented. How are you going to mingle the two, or are you setting up a separate corporation to work with Demonstration Cities?

MAYOR CAVANAGH: It is a separate corporation. We think that eventually the Industrial Development Corporation, which has now really—I won't say outlived its usefulness—but has really achieved some of its initial objectives, could well eventually be absorbed by this new corporation. There is still money in the Industrial Development Corporation and practically all of the same people are involved—the same business and labor interests. I think there is about a quarter of a million dollars still left in the Industrial Development Corporation. We will probably end up dissolving it and transferring its assets into the new corporation.

The Industrial Development Corporation's purpose was really to act as sort of a catalyst. As you know, at the time the Area Redevelopment Act was passed, its purpose was to try and generate more job opportunities in these so-called depressed areas. One of the requirements of the Act was that if a man wanted a loan, say, through the Area Redevelopment Administration, and could establish the fact that this loan in turn would create more job opportunities, he had to have at least 10% local financing. In many instances, these were not the kinds of loans that the conventional financial institutions looked too kindly upon. That was his problem, of course. Here we were with a number of people that had business propositions which probably would generate a number of jobs, yet they couldn't get loans in the normal, conventional way. So, it was necessary to create a third force.

The manner in which it loaned money was sort of interesting. It was similar to the old RFC. If I came to them for a loan, they would give me a loan but in turn I'd have to commit myself to selling the debentures which were issued as a result of that loan. It was really sort of a transmission belt for money, but it still qualified under the law.

There were a number of new hotels and motels which were subject to some criticism, I might say, by some members of the Congress. They felt this really hadn't generated the kinds of jobs that the Congress had contemplated when they adopted the ARA Act. The fact of the matter was that they did generate a tremendous number of jobs in a relatively new industry in Detroit—the service industry—which has become quite a large industry as a result of a new convention business which we have in Detroit. We built a big convention hall with which I am sure many of you are familiar. We had an inadequate number of hotel and motel rooms, and our service industry was woefully deficient. We needed new hotel and motel rooms, new restaurants, and things like that. The ARA Act assisted in the creation of some of these facilities. It also assisted in the creation of some new research laboratories and things of that nature as well.

QUESTION: I would like to know if you have a citizen review board for police brutality cases, and what your opinion is as to the use of that sort of thing for communication between the depressed area and the police.

MAYOR CAVANAGH: As every politician says, "I'm glad you asked that question." I really am not, but I'll answer it. It doesn't bother me. I answered it yesterday.

I am opposed to a police review board. I've stated my opposition to it consistently for a number of years—prior to my election, as a matter of fact. I'm sure some of my constituents didn't believe that I really felt that way. But I do, principally because I think it's a device that political figures sometimes use to duck behind. It has no real authority, no responsibility. Under our charter, even if I created one, the responsibility for the conduct of our police department is vested in our police commissioner and the mayor. The mayor appoints the commissioner. It's very simple, at least to me it seems simple, that if our police department is not responsive, as it should be, then there is a manner in which the community may respond. I think to some degree in 1961 it did. There were many people who questioned the operation of the police department, and I'm sure I was the beneficiary of some of those questions at election time.

We have in Michigan a State Civil Rights Commission. This acts almost like a review board because any citizen that feels aggrieved by any action of any public official, be that official a policeman, a mayor, or anybody else, can file a complaint with the Michigan Civil Rights Commission and that Commission, under the law, has to hold hearings and make some public determination.

We also have a mechanism which I created within the police department, called a Citizen's Complaint Bureau, that operates rather independently within the department. It's true that it is an adjunct of the department. It has to investigate every complaint made by every citizen. It used to be that some superintendent or deputy superintendent of police would make the decision as to which complaints went to the Citizen's Complaint Bureau and which didn't—which was a sort of self-serving system. But now any complaint that's made has to be investigated. They in turn have to make a recommendation directly to the police commissioner. It operates right under the commissioner.

I've also charged our Commission on Community Relations, which is a citizen body dealing with human relations and community relations, with the job of overviewing the operation of our Citizen's Complaint Bureau within the police department. I have instructed them carefully that if the Citizen's Complaint Bureau is not fulfilling the charge which I have extended to it, then that fact is to be reported to me and to be reported publicly. Involved in the Commission on Community Relations are a number of our civil rights organizations, so they have almost constant and immediate access to the investigative procedure of our police department. I'm not saying they are all happy and satisfied with it, but the interesting thing has been that no one has claimed that this Citizen's Complaint Bureau, as of late at least, has whitewashed any case of alleged police brutality.

* * *

Remarks by John T. Ryan, Jr.

President, Mine Safety Appliances Company

Earlier this month you probably read the story about the Pennsylvania Railroad's dramatic plans to reclaim 148 acres of blight in downtown Pittsburgh and in a bordering district of commercial slums and redevelop it into an ultra-modern business-residential complex built around a Transport Center.

This announcement has once again focused nationwide attention on Pittsburgh and its renaissance. So from my point of view the timing to speak on urban development in Pittsburgh is ideal and I welcome the opportunity to share the experiences some of us have had in the fascinating challenge of rebuilding an older city. I am hopeful that this story will be helpful to you in your efforts to improve life in your various home communities.

For the past twenty years Pittsburgh's rebirth has been told in countless newspaper stories, magazines, and publications in this country and abroad, and has brought a steady stream of visitors and delegations from every part of the United States and from throughout the world.

They have come not only to see what has been accomplished but, more importantly, to find out how it was done and judge whether the same methods and techniques could work in their respective cities.

In my remarks today, I shall cover briefly first two points— what has been accomplished and how it was done. As to the third point—the application to your city—I shall share some observations with you and outline some of the principles and policies that have worked successfully in our renaissance and leave the final judgment as to exportability to you.

Let's approach Pittsburgh as an HBS[3] case study. Pittsburgh came out of World War II with a bleak outlook. Smoke and smog blanketed the city. Floods were a constant threat. The rivers and streams were virtually open sewers into which municipalities and industries poured their raw wastes. No limited access highways existed and only one was in design. There was a woeful lack of recreational opportunities, and the housing inventory was as poor as in any American city—with more than 60% of the existing housing over 50 years old.

Urban blight was all around us, and particularly critical in the Golden Triangle—the city's compact central business district that

---

[3] Harvard Business School.

is so essential to the economic well-being of the region and as the main tax base for the city, county, and school district.

Mass transportation, if it deserved that name, was nothing more than a hodge-podge of independent private carriers, operating without uniform fares, scheduling, or transfer privileges and often with obsolete equipment. There was no plan for unification—to say nothing of plans for rapid mass transit.

For years our city had been the brunt of jokes—from the nickname Smoky City to the alleged remark by the famous architect, the late Frank Lloyd Wright, that the best thing to do with Pittsburgh was to abandon the place.

Economically, too, the outlook was dark. Many of the large corporations that had long been headquartered in Pittsburgh were considering moving elsewhere—because of this environment I've described and because of the increasing difficulty of attracting managerial, engineering, and scientific personnel. Simply stated, the wives of prospective executives didn't want to live and raise their families under these prevailing conditions.

Well, what did we in the business community do about it? More than a hundred large industrial firms are headquartered in Pittsburgh. Our company, which manufactures equipment to save lives, has a market wherever people work, and its operations are worldwide. We could move away and locate elsewhere, as many other Pittsburgh-based firms could.

In Pittsburgh, as World War II was ending, we decided to stay and rebuild—as did most of the industrial and business leadership.

As a whole group of younger leaders returned from the war and came into positions of executive responsibility and power, these men resolved to tackle the city's myriad of problems.

Under the leadership of Richard K. Mellon, the Allegheny Conference on Community Development was formed in 1943 and incorporated as a nonprofit, nonpartisan, privately financed citizens' organization. It was created to marshal the full energies and resources of the community behind a bold and imaginative community development and improvement program and provide a vehicle in which business could participate actively in this area.

Some 100 persons serve in this citizens' organization, representing a cross-section of leadership in industry, business, finance, commerce, labor, education, public administration, and civic affairs.

About the first thing the Allegheny Conference did was to establish a close working relationship with the elected public officials. The Conference recognized from the very beginning that the most ambitious plans conceivable could not be carried out unless they had the backing and support of local government. More about this point later, however.

Before highlighting what has been accomplished in Pittsburgh during the past two decades, I would call your attention to the tremendous public investments that have already been made in your city and in every other American city. For this reason alone, cities must be reclaimed, rebuilt, and restored to robust health. We cannot afford to do otherwise.

The replacement cost of public facilities in Pittsburgh alone would exceed $2.5 billion. Personally, I think this is a very conservative estimate, in view of the high cost of construction today. This estimate of $2.5 billion is based on the assessed valuation of tax-exempt property within the city of Pittsburgh and includes the valuation of just the public facilities, such as the buildings of the four levels of government located within the city, public schools, public housing units, public garages and sanitary facilities, the public utilities, the 2,300 acres of city parks and playgrounds, the highways and city streets, the water lines and lighting, public transit, and the public hospitals and charitable institutions. Even in an affluent society, $2.5 billion is a lot of money and, furthermore, I'm positive the replacement of these facilities in Pittsburgh would cost much more than that.

Now as to what has been accomplished in Pittsburgh during the past two decades.

Smoke has been cleared from the skies and today Pittsburgh and Allegheny County are covered by one of the most effective air pollution control ordinances in the country. A series of flood control reservoirs, built by the federal government, protect Pittsburgh and the entire Upper Ohio Valley from serious floods.

A $100 million sewage treatment system has been in operation since 1959, improving greatly the quality of the water in our rivers and streams and opening them up for recreation.

More than one-fourth of the Golden Triangle has been rebuilt and redeveloped, including 60 acres at the Point, where the Allegheny and Monongahela Rivers join to form the Ohio and where Pittsburgh was first settled over 200 years ago.

Two downtown projects deserve particular mention. Gateway Center, a new business and commercial district adjoining Point State Park in the Point area, was the first redevelopment venture in this country to direct major public-private action to the critical problem of downtown blight. Here the Equitable Life Assurance Society, as the redeveloper, now has an investment of over $135 million in this complex.

The other is Mellon Square which paved the way for the reconstruction of the midtown Triangle. Three Mellon foundations gave the city sufficient funds to acquire a square block of blight, demolish the old structures, and build a beautiful park, which has an underground garage beneath. This was the key to assuring the construction of the Alcoa skyscraper and the 40-story Mellon-U.S. Steel building.

A major expressway, the Penn-Lincoln Parkway, also provides the Triangle with a direct connection to the Turnpike on the east and the multi-million dollar Greater Pittsburgh Airport on the west.

Some thirty private mass transit carriers have been consolidated into a single, unified system under the Port Authority of Allegheny County, and a rapid transit study is under way. Through the Public Parking Authority a series of downtown garages have been constructed and metered parking lots built in other business sections of the city.

Recreational opportunities have been vastly enlarged. Millions of dollars have been poured into our colleges and universities and into our Health Center. Increased funds for public education have been secured through a vigorous civic effort which resulted in the legislature revising the state formula for aid to the major cities in Pennsylvania. We now have 150 research facilities employing over

20,000 professional and skilled people in the nine counties of western Pennsylvania.

A promising start has been made through ACTION-Housing, Inc., a private, nonprofit civic organization, in building sales and rental housing for families of moderate means. The Regional Industrial Development Corporation of Southwestern Pennsylvania was formed to foster economic growth, and its record of accomplishments is indeed impressive.

I think you will agree that the past two decades have been exciting, productive, and fruitful years in Pittsburgh. Yet, I am glad to say that there is an impatience in the New Pittsburgh, a feeling that only a good beginning has been made—a keen desire to move on with the job and win new laurels in this challenging field of urban renewal and resolve the many other shortcomings that all our cities have.

What are the ideas, principles and ingredients that are responsible for whatever success Pittsburgh has enjoyed?

First, it seems to me that there must be a focus of power of such strength and authority that the top leadership of the city—business and political—has a rallying point that gives the program continuing, uninterrupted support. It cannot be a sporadic approach.

Certainly, the citizens' organization spearheading the movement must be genuinely and truly nonpartisan. Partisan politics has no place in this field. The members of the action agency must be a dedicated group, sincerely and deeply concerned about their city and its future. They must really care and be willing to do something about it.

As I mentioned earler, there has to be mutual trust and respect between the business leaders and the elected public officials—a rapport that, like Caesar's wife, is above suspicion. It must be clearly understood that no individual or group will ever attempt to use the central action agency for personal, corporate, or political gain.

The central action agency must not impose its ideas or plans. Its role is to enlist the full energies and resources of the community behind its program.

Private action groups must never forget that they cannot enact or legislate. For the exercise of government the citizenry must, very properly, look to the elected officials who are given the public responsibility of legislation and administration.

A partnership between business leadership and the elected public officials that creates the climate and atmosphere conducive to wholehearted cooperation and support is a cardinal principle for success in this pioneering work.

I referred earlier to the formation of the Allegheny Conference on Community Development in 1943 and the cross-section of leadership that comprises its membership of some 100 persons, whom we call "sponsors." The sponsors, by the very nature of their affiliations, can effectively generate action in many situations. You will find many of them serving by appointment of the local public official on the various boards, authorities, and commissions that have been created to carry out the Pittsburgh development program. They serve without compensation and bring a wealth of talent and experience to these quasi-legal bodies that government couldn't afford to hire.

These sponsors elect a small executive committee that is the policy-making body of the Allegheny Conference. It meets regularly, on the third Monday of each month.

There is one rule that is absolutely necessary to the success of an organization like the Allegheny Conference—no substitutes; no delegation of civic responsibility to others. Only the person elected to this executive committee may serve. It is interesting to note that no person has ever refused to serve and that the attendance at these monthly meetings is amazingly high.

When Equitable Life was wrapping up the Gateway Center project in 1949, the insurance company's top executives felt that at least 60% of the rental space in the projected three office towers should be under lease prior to start of construction. This was done at an executive committee meeting of the Allegheny Conference, and Equitable Life secured 20-year leases for more than 60% of the space before a spade of dirt had been turned. I submit that only the top executives can make these kinds of important decisions that can have such far-reaching effects in the life of a city.

The central action agency must also know when and where to exercise its power and influence and it should never undertake a project that has no chance of success.

Citizens' groups sometimes tend to get away out in front on blue-sky projects that are frequently impractical, unattainable, and are doomed to failure from the beginning. Proper timing and the common sense to know when and where to use power and leverage are of overriding importance and also a great responsibility. Sound planning is essential.

Today the Allegheny Conference is solidly behind a number of projects that it could not have supported 10 or 15 years ago. The central action agency must be as fluid and flexible as the times in which it works. The emphasis will change from time to time but the objective will always remain the same.

I believe that it is also extremely important to develop a full-time, competent staff in the private and public agencies involved in this urban activity. It is no place for nepotism or to take care of good old "Joe" whom you didn't want in the firm. A professional staff that knows its business and is on top of the program day in and day out is the only way to meet the challenge of the urban scene these days.

This professional staff should also have quick and easy access to the heads of industry and business and their immediate operating executives for counsel and advice—just as the lines of communication to the top city officials must be constantly open. Immediate access to top management must be possible, because time is often the determining factor in whether an agreement can be consummated.

Modern management and business techniques must also be employed in the private and public urban renewal agencies. The growing complexity of the planning and redevelopment process demands it. Pittsburgh's Urban Redevelopment Authority is big business. Today the private investment alone in the Authority's 20 projects that have been completed or are under way exceeds $500 million.

Another principle of the Allegheny Conference since its incorporation is worth serious consideration, although in some communities the opposite approach may be desirable. It has been the policy to keep the Allegheny Conference as the central guiding, coordinating, and action agency, and when the need arises to tackle special problem areas such as housing, economic development, recreation and conservation, a spin-off is effected.

Several examples will underscore the Conference's thinking.

As the urban renewal program gathered momentum, the problem of increasing the supply of moderate-cost housing for families in the $5,000 to $8,000 income bracket threatened to slow down our efforts. Families in the upper economic range can look to the private market to supply their housing needs, and through the public housing authorities the lower income families are being taken care of—even though here the demand frequently exceeds the supply and the traditional form of public housing leaves much to be desired, especially in design.

The crucial housing shortage, however, exists in the moderate range.

A study financed by the Allegheny Conference led to the formation of ACTION-Housing, Inc. in 1957, as a private, nonprofit civic organization to work with all elements of the housing industry —builders, realtors, labor, mortgage firms, the 129 various municipalities in Allegheny County and all other housing interests. Its goals were threefold:

(1) To increase the supply of good new housing available to families of moderate income through private enterprise;
(2) To bring about modernization of older housing and the revitalization of declining neighborhoods;
(3) To develop a research base for future housing and urban renewal programs.

One of ACTION-Housing's first accomplishments was to create the Pittsburgh Development Fund, a $1.6 million revolving loan fund to provide equity capital—seed money—for the development of new housing and the modernization of existing housing. The Fund was established through interest-bearing loans and grants from 30 banks, utility companies, corporations, department stores, and foundations. The Fund has loaned out $430,000—$206,000 of which has been paid back.

To date the Fund is bringing about the building of $11 million worth of private enterprise housing in Pittsburgh. The first housing development undertaken by ACTION-Housing, Inc. was East Hills Park, which will eventually have 1,200 cluster-planned townhouses and apartments, embodying new concepts in design, land use, financing, labor contracts and legal procedures—all of which greatly reduce loan and closing costs.

The 187 dwelling units completed are all sold or rented and occupied, and very shortly construction will start on 130 rental townhouses and 283 rental apartments. A second housing development has been virtually completed in another section of the city—Sheraden Park, consisting of 188 cooperative townhouses.

In the Homewood-Brushton section of Pittsburgh, where our company's headquarters and plant operations are located, AC-TION-Housing, Inc. launched an urban extension program to arrest the decline and deterioration of this older neighborhood and transform it into a well-ordered and revitalized community. Some of us met, helped create the Homewood-Brushton Citizens Renewal Council, formulated a far-reaching rejuvenation program, raised some money from the companies in the area, applied for and received a grant from the Buhl Foundation of Pittsburgh—all of which was matched by The Ford Foundation which was deeply interested in this pilot demonstration.

I am pleased to tell you that already remarkable results have been achieved in Homewood-Brushton and this community is definitely on its way back. Selected demolition of abandoned houses, modernization of older but structurally sound homes, provision of several parking lots, a revised traffic pattern, a number of playgrounds and athletic fields, have all contributed to its "new look."

Another private renaissance agency created to deal solely with the area of economic development, which, of course, involves the fabric of the entire region, is the Regional Industrial Development Corporation of Southwestern Pennsylvania.

Formed in 1955 following a study undertaken by the Allegheny Conference and reorganized in 1962, RIDC is at work broadening the area's economic base, assisting firms that need new facilities with financing and technical "know-how" and developing at a cost of $10 million in land and buildings the region's largest, fully planned industrial park. The corporation has also been attracting wholly new enterprises to the southwestern Pennsylvania district—enterprises in the field of nuclear energy, electronics, aerospace, and scientific instrumentation. These are growth situations and industries that Pittsburgh never had before.

During its brief history, RIDC itself has created two new vehicles—the RIDC Industrial Development Fund and the RIDC Real Estate Company—both of which help growth situations with financial assistance and the selection of attractive sites.

The RIDC Industrial Development Fund has made more than 85 loan commitments in an aggregate amount of $8.6 million and created at least 3,500 new jobs in the past few years. Many millions of dollars more have been generated from conventional financial avenues and channeled into these new enterprises as a result of the RIDC Fund.

A year or so ago RIDC formed a Scientific and Research Advisory Group that has been instrumental in laying the foundation for a rapid transit industry in the Pittsburgh area. This group played an important role in organizing the first International Conference on Urban Transportation which was held in Pittsburgh last February 1, 2, and 3. As a result of that highly successful conference, a Transportation Research Institute has been established at Carnegie Institute of Technology. Its purpose is to engage in broad research studies, with immediate emphasis on rapid transit and high-speed interurban transportation. Seed money for the initial operations of the Institute came in the form of a grant of $300,000 from the Richard King Mellon Foundation.

Robert H. Ryan, a graduate of Harvard College and the Harvard Graduate School of Business Administration, is the president of RIDC.

Another spin-off example is the Western Pennsylvania Conservancy—again a nonprofit citizens' organization dedicated to the acquisition and preservation of significant conservation areas and the development of outdoor recreation sites throughout our part of Pennsylvania.

Through Conservancy programs nearly 35,000 acres have been set aside for recreation and conservation purposes, with more than

18,000 acres acquired directly. Several new state parks have been created out of this land reserve bank—including Ohiopyle State Park, an 18,000–acre woodland only 45 miles from downtown Pittsburgh and Moraine State Park now under construction to the north of the city in Butler County.

How are new programs initiated and launched? This question is asked many times over, and it is a good one.

In reviewing the initial financing of many of our programs that are now a brilliant success on the Pittsburgh regional scene and are so significant to the long-term hopes and aspirations of the community, it is surprising what a relatively small amount of seed money was actually required to start some of these programs rolling.

In 1946 when Pittsburgh's Urban Redevelopment Authority was created by action of the mayor and city council, there were no funds to operate the new agency and none were in sight. The Honorable David L. Lawrence was then mayor of the city and had ingeniously appointed three Republican business leaders out of five members to the nonpaid Authority Board because he felt that the Republicans might have better luck with potential redevelopers with money to invest. Not to be outdone, the Republicans recognized that any redevelopment proposals would require full support in City Hall; so at their request and insistence, the mayor became chairman of the Authority, a position he held through his terms as mayor of Pittsburgh, as governor of Pennsylvania, and now as the chairman of the President's Committee on Equal Opportunity in Housing. And how fortunate Pittsburgh has been to have a political statesman of his stature in that command post.

This top-level board still had no money to operate the Authority and the board didn't want to ask City Council for an appropriation, since there was no assurance that a project could be put together.

Several Pittsburgh businessmen personally guaranteed on faith a $50,000 bond issue to get the Authority off the ground.

Furthermore, the Redevelopment Authority has never had to make a request to City Council for an operation appropriation. Through redevelopment fees paid by private developers, the

Authority has been able to fund its operations on nonfederal projects.

The seed money of $50,000, which was repaid in full, fostered a program that has grown into 20 redevelopment projects embracing 1,600 acres throughout the city, with a private investment of an astounding $500 million in new buildings.

WQED—Channel 13, the country's first community-sponsored educational television station, was born in Pittsburgh and has been on the air since April, 1954. Three foundations made seed grants totaling $350,000 for the necessary equipment to begin operations. Westinghouse Broadcasting Company gave the use of its FM tower and the Pittsburgh Plate Glass Company conveyed a deed to the University of Pittsburgh for WQED's present studio. Friends of WQED contributed $335,000 in a public fund-raising drive and the station was a going concern.

Today WQED is on the air an average of 97 hours a week except in summer months when programming is somewhat curtailed. The station serves a signal area of over 2.5 million people with in-school programs at the elementary, secondary, and college levels and a wide selection of cultural, informative, and entertaining programs for adults.

WQED now has an annual budget of over $900,000 and is currently embarked on a $5 million capital improvement program. Of this amount, $3.5 million has already been committed. The Richard K. Mellon Foundation made a grant of $1.5 million last December and The Ford Foundation will contribute $2 million under a recently announced program of matching grants to the nation's educational television stations.

WQED has already made an extraordinary contribution to the enrichment of life in the Pittsburgh region and I am sure that its possibilities are unlimited.

Pittsburgh's public and private leadership has not been afraid to use new tools to carry out ideas and programs or to invent new ones when old methods just wouldn't work. That is why the Regional Industrial Development Corporation, ACTION-Housing, Inc. and the Western Pennsylvania Conservancy were created and why the most recent addition to the civic family—the Southwestern

Pennsylvania Regional Planning Commission—has been established.

Last month the Pittsburgh City Council, on the recommendation of Mayor Joseph M. Barr, established another new tool—a $6 million residential land fund to acquire sites for moderate and low income housing. The fund will enable the city's Urban Redevelopment Authority to purchase, sell, lease, transfer or hold sites for residential developments and the fund can be used independently or may be supplemented with city, state, federal, or private grants.

A new multi-purpose Civic Arena was desperately needed to serve as an amphitheater in summer for civic light opera and as a sports palace and convention hall. To build and operate this unique facility, the Public Auditorium Authority of Pittsburgh and Allegheny County was created. The Civic Arena is a reality and is to Pittsburgh what the Empire State Building and Eiffel Tower are to New York and Paris.

What about exportability? Will the Pittsburgh tools and techniques work successfully elsewhere?

Of course, most cities now have redevelopment authorities and other public and private agencies concerned with economic growth, housing, downtown development and the myriad of other problems facing urban centers these days. Many of the ideas that Pittsburgh has pioneered with have already been used in other cities.

I think that a transplant in its entirety is not likely to succeed because cities, like each of us, are all different and have their own distinctive characteristics. The idea or the new tool should be adapted and modeled, I think, to suit the needs and conditions that may confront your community.

With the record of accomplishments and achievements of the last 20 years behind us, you may be wondering whether the Pittsburgh renaissance hasn't run out of steam.

The program actually gathers and gains momentum all the time. There are many more projects in the pipeline today than there were 20 years ago.

Chatham Center—a $26 million complex consisting of an apartment tower, an office building crowned by an 11-story motor lodge, all built on top of a 2,200-car garage—is nearing completion in the Upper Triangle.

Ground will be broken this summer for Pittsburgh's new stadium on an 87-acre site on the North Side across from Point State Park and Gateway Center. An aquarium at the Pittsburgh Zoo is under construction. Plans for a Center for the Arts with a magnificent Symphony Hall as the centerpiece are moving forward.

During the next 18 months, construction of 6 major office buildings is projected for downtown Pittsburgh—creating approximately 4 million additional square feet of office space.

Private enterprise and government have the tools to reshape and bring new vigor to our cities. Each of us has an obligation to do his part in "proportion to the bounties that nature measured to him." This is Jefferson democracy at its finest and indeed the compelling challenge of the hour.

DISCUSSION FOLLOWING MR. RYAN'S REMARKS

QUESTION: I'm from Cleveland, Mr. Ryan, and one of the things I've observed in our city is that the city seems in-grown. Everybody is so busy doing everything that nobody has time to do anything. The question that I would like to ask is: how did you break up this in-grown character of the top social structure of the city and get this thing started? We don't have a Mellon.

MR. RYAN: Well, you have four or five reasonable substitutes, I think.

Let me say that I wasn't there at the very start. Certainly General Mellon embraced this program wholeheartedly and saw that it was carried through. In the intervening years, based possibly on the initial start, you generate a feeling and an enthusiasm among people that this is one of their major responsibilities. Every one of us in this room has a myriad of responsibilities. So, therefore, I think you have to be selective. You have to give an order of priorities to things. You establish the standard that only the top, chief executive of a company can serve; that he can have no substitute. Pittsburgh is perhaps more closely knit business-wise than many other cities. This has helped in Pittsburgh. I am sure that we have been extremely fortunate in the fact that service of this kind to this type of top-level action organization—and this is an action organization—has been accepted as certainly the number one or number two priority.

QUESTION: Mr. Ryan, how are you going to go about tackling the mass transportation problem?

MR. RYAN: There is a man in the back of the room who can handle this a lot better than I can. Bob Ryan has really gone after this program and has prodded all of us and used every means of public and private communication available. Bob has done a real job in getting the political structure to recognize the need for this program—getting assistance from the federal funds and the state funds and anybody that can contribute something to this.

Pittsburgh has a great economic asset in the development of transportation with people like U.S. Steel and Allegheny Ludlum and the Aluminum Company and Westinghouse and Westinghouse Airbrake, and so forth.

Bob was largely instrumental in having the first International Conference on Transportation in Pittsburgh last February. Out of that, for example, came a grant from one of the foundations for a $300,000 program at Carnegie Institute of Technology.

We have under way a study—by the same group that did the San Francisco Bay Area Transportation Study—a long-range program for implementation of mass rapid transit in Pittsburgh, which certainly is essential if our type of city with our topography is going to grow.

CHAPTER III

President Johnson's Address

Delivered by John W. Macy, Jr.

The greatness and growth of this country and its cities have been built on individual initiative and private enterprise. We have profound belief in the sacredness of free private decisions, at the polling place and in the marketplace.

These are the firm foundations upon which our freedom rests. These are the sources of the energy and creativity which have made ours a nation blessed with abundance beyond any in the long chronicles of human strivings for the good things of life.

Now, as in the past, the progress and stability of our free society have been firmly rooted in a harmonious and creative partnership of public and private actions, and the constructive cooperation of public and private institutions.

We can be justly proud of our unparalleled accomplishments. But we cannot be content. We cannot relax in contemplation of a great past. We must meet the challenges of the future.

These are times of rapid technological change. These are times of even more rapid social change.

These changes have consequences so far-reaching and profound that they both threaten and challenge the social and political institutions which we revere, and upon which our society is built.

One of the gravest challenges, one of the greatest opportunities, which this time of rapid social change offers us is the issue you are discussing here today. It is the rapid and accelerating urbanization of our society.

In another generation nearly 200 million people will live an urban life. In the next ten years three out of every four Americans will be living in urban areas. The issue before us is whether this development of massive metropolitan concentrations—which is already in process—will be the foundation of a better America. Along with a concern for the sheer quantity of life in the urban society, we must be concerned with its quality if the Great Society is to be truly capable of greatness.

American business has a large stake in solving the problems of urbanization. For cities are the places where the markets are. Cities are the places where commerce and trade—manufacturing and distribution—take place. Cities are the places where the labor force lives, where it must rely on systems of urban transportation to travel to and from work. Cities are the places where the chaos or serenity of the worker's environment affects his productivity and morale. The city is the great and complex organism in which business and production must be carried out. If the city is inefficient, doing business is inefficient and costly.

While the nation has been making giant strides in space and defense technology, our cities are still operating with many of the same techniques and traditional assumptions they have used for decades. It is not necessary to do more than list a few of the many neglected areas in our domestic society: poor schools, inadequate medical care, air and water pollution, traffic congestion, run-down housing, formless urban sprawl, and human deprivation. Currently, large expenditures are made to mitigate these conditions, but relatively little effort is being made to find new or improved ways of attaining long-range urban objectives, either by the federal, state, or local governments. This situation must be changed if our cities are to reap the benefits that can be provided by American ingenuity.

There is a rising desire on the part of urban leadership to search out new and better ways for attacking the problems of city management, planning, and resource allocation. However, in terms of magnitude of the problems, too few imaginative people from many different disciplines have been mobilized to find new approaches.

New ways of meeting urban needs are likely to grow out of existing technology that is not currently being applied to, or developed for, urban problems. There are numerous cases where the technology is already at hand but is awaiting a demonstration of its practicality and the creation of a market. One contribution the federal government can make is in helping to overcome the reluctance to accept promising innovations by making possible their demonstration and evaluation.

Usually, major new applications of existing technology cannot proceed directly from conception to full-scale operation without passing through a period of experimentation and demonstration. However, for large-scale systems, the cost of such demonstrations sometimes will be beyond the capabilities of either private industry or the local municipalities, and federal support or matching grants will be required. Selective federal assistance to private firms or city governments wishing to invest in promising new facilities or methods, and the rigorous evaluation of these efforts, would provide those facing similar investment decisions with the information needed to make informed judgments.

To deal effectively with the great problems which confront our urban society will require a vast application of resources, energy, and leadership.

It will test the capacity of our present institutions, both public and private.

It will require new and imaginative ways of combining our public and private skills and institutions.

It will require the emergence of new, yet unborn institutions and working relations.

It will, indeed, test to the utmost the resources and the resourcefulness of our pluralistic democratic society.

It will test its capacity to adapt and to respond to new problems with new forms and new solutions.

The private business community, and the leaders of American business can participate with government at all levels in devising and bringing into being the flexible, creative new relationships and instruments. An even more effective partnership for urban progress can be activated.

This partnership is, as *Fortune* magazine recently calls it, "the new interdependence" and is based on wide areas of mutual interest. These areas must be broadened and deepened if the interdependence is to be of lasting benefit for all Americans. A genuine cooperative approach to the complex problems of the urban environment serves both the public good and private enterprise.

Government services feed the roots of our society. Schools and hospitals, parks and highways, clean rivers and pure air—these are vital ingredients of the good society. Business and industry could not flourish without them. Moreover, government could not provide them without the aid of business.

Your taxes help to pay for these things. But taxes should not and cannot be the whole extent of your contribution. Just as rich and mutually rewarding to the whole American society are the enlightened works of business alone.

Your laboratories help to probe the mysteries of our universe and the secrets of human life. Your conservation practices can help to restore our rivers, clean our smog-laden air, protect the beauty of the American landscape. Your concern for the safety of your products, whether aspirin or automobiles, can help to prevent human suffering and loss of life. Your open employment policies can help to erase the blot of racial discrimination. Your training programs add to our total education effort. Your pensions, together with the government social insurance programs, protect the economic security of millions and, not incidentally, also serve as a powerful stabilizing force for the entire business community.

Even your criticism is an asset to government. When you point out ways in which government can better serve our free enterprise economy, we listen attentively. For the true interests of business lie in advancing the public good, and those are also the interests of your government.

The rising and inescapable tide of urbanization is bringing with it two dire and drastic problems—the problems of urban decay and the problems of urban growth.

The hearts of our cities are rotting.

The human cost of urban decay is high and alarming.

The poor, the disadvantaged, the discriminated against are increasingly concentrated into tight, squalid ghettos—deprived of a decent environment, with little opportunity and less hope. This is the grey, ill-prepared, tragic driftwood of our otherwise affluent society.

We must concentrate every available resource—in planning, in housing construction, in job training, in health facilities, in recreation, in welfare programs, in education—to improve dramatically the living conditions of the urban poor.

This will require a great and concerted effort on the part of local leadership, both public and private.

The Demonstration Cities Bill which the President has presented to the Congress this year is designed to provide the means and the incentive to focus the techniques and talents within our society on this pressing crisis of the American City. Nothing less than an all-out, comprehensive, and determined assault on this problem will do.

The second great problem which threatens the American City is the problem of overwhelming growth. Growth is a mark of strength in cities as in business, and reflects increasing opportunities. But growth if uncontrolled and haphazard will deprive our cities of the very benefits it attempts to offer.

We cannot afford to despoil our precious land with urban scatter-ation which is without reason or form, without efficiency or economy, and clearly without beauty.

We must find ways to direct and shape the patterns of urban growth so that communities emerge which will improve the quality of urban life—communities which give proper regard to the appropriate and efficient relationships between houses, shops, places of employment, transportation, health, recreation and cultural facilities.

We need to build communities in which people of all economic and social levels can live and find opportunity and enrichment.

We need to build communities which are not wasteful of our precious and limited resources—whether they be the beauties of natural scenery and our pure and once-pure water and air, or the costly structures of our cities, their highways and their water and sewer lines.

We need to develop urban transportation systems which will

lessen the cost, in money, time and frustration, of taking advantage of the opportunities of our cities. We must do this without carelessly destroying the very human values they are supposed to serve.

The key to orderly urban growth is good planning (which you practice in administering modern business enterprises) effectuated, in this case, by the public and private actions which will make the plan become reality.

The proposed program for demonstrations in effective metropolitan planning will provide a new thrust and new opportunities. It will encourage cities throughout the country to shape their futures through planning which is not only comprehensive but practical, not only farsighted but geared to immediate public and private actions.

The response of the businessman of America to the staggering problems of urbanization is not just a dream, or a pious wish. It is already beginning to happen.

Let me give you some examples.

In New York City, federal and local government, private foundations, settlement houses and churches, along with private builders and real estate firms, have combined their resources to give rehabilitated housing and new hope to deprived families living in New York's old-law tenements. Pioneering methods in rehabilitation can bring into being a whole new industry of suppliers, managers, builders and credit institutions.

In Tulsa, Oklahoma, a group of homebuilders joined forces with the federal government and local welfare agencies to develop a housing project designed to give the poor the opportunity to live in decent housing and, after social and job training, to lift themselves up the economic and social ladder to the point where they could realize the dream of most Americans—to own his own home.

In Oakland, California, the Economic Development Administration of the Commerce Department is investing $23 million to stimulate economic development and create some 2,500 new jobs. Concurrently, the business community in Oakland is raising $1.5 million on their own to complement the federal government effort.

Throughout the country, businessmen are serving on local urban renewal commissions, public housing commissions, and city planning commissions. Indeed, a survey conducted in 1964 showed that businessmen make up a preponderant proportion of those citizens who serve their communities on planning commissions. They bring to these social undertakings the realism, energy, and competence which our business leadership possesses in such abundance.

The urban society which can bring together public and private action to achieve efficient, orderly urban growth may have met, and conquered, the greatest challenger of creative federalism.

To create urban community while solving urban problems, creative federalism must be informed and enlivened by consensual democracy. The concept of consensual democracy recognizes that the American people are not now divided along any deep lines of economic class or social groups. All of you present here today do have special viewpoints concerning the city that emerge from your jobs and experiences. But the differences between your interests and those of other groups—employees, public servants, consumers—are indeed small compared to the convergence of all-out interests in solving the city's problems.

Most of our citizens share the same goals, the same vision, of what our society should become. There are no sharp issues that divide us in our common effort to raise the quality of the urban environment.

Therefore, the particular interests of businessmen will be benefited by the increasing good health and growth of our cities. But, more important, as citizens of our consensual democracy you have the same great interest in the health of our cities as any other citizen.

The problems which our rapidly urbanizing society faces are many and grave. The challenges which it presents are great. We will meet these challenges—for we must. In responding to this challenge, I am confident that the businessmen of America will discharge their proper role—just as they have at so many other grave moments in our country's history.

CHAPTER IV

Housing and Urban Renewal

The discussion on housing and urban renewal focused primarily on the business-government relationship. It began with a venting of frustrations on both sides. Gradually it shifted to the future and to how both parties might be induced to work more effectively together. A number of specific suggestions were made as to organizations, programs, and incentives. They point the way toward a significantly different approach to the city's housing and renewal problems in future years.

As in all the discussions, the background paper served as the main common denominator, and it will be presented first. Following this paper will be excerpts from the comments of both businessmen and government officials. Finally, we will turn to the new programs and the new approaches which are currently in the conceptual or experimental stage, but which may significantly shape the future.

Background Paper

Of the various topics being discussed at the conference, business probably has had a more active interest and involvement in housing and urban renewal than in any other. As developers, contractors, and lenders businessmen have been engaged directly in renewal projects. The bulk of the funds going into housing and urban renewal are still private funds despite the bewildering array of federal programs in this area. Beyond direct participation, many business firms and businessmen have been active and vocal in the planning process. What have been the results of this business participation, what are the chances for its continuation, and what are the federal programs which are likely to determine the future direction of urban housing and renewal?

Over the last decade federal activity in the housing and urban renewal areas has expanded, rising from $314 million in 1956 to $2 billion in 1966. This federal activity is small, however, by comparison with the $71 billion of new construction put in place in 1965 by all sources.

Of the $71 billion expended on construction in 1965, urban renewal accounts for roughly $4 billion. Of this $4 billion, approximately 17% is federally funded, indicating that the federal government is inclined and/or forced to play a greater role in central city projects than in the construction field as a whole.

On the housing side, of the 1.52 million nonfarm housing starts in 1965, 1.48 million (or 97%) were privately owned, with .04 million in public hands. Of the private starts, 83% were financed conventionally, and 17% were FHA or VA insured.

One of the more significant discoveries made by the federal government during its experimentation with renewal projects was that coordinated attacks on specific blighted urban areas were far more effective per dollar spent than a package of uncoordinated projects spread throughout a city. As a result, the Johnson Administration has proposed the Demonstration Cities Bill. A summary of this Bill is found in Appendix A. Briefly, the Bill offers attractive financial support to any city that is willing to focus its attention on a single, "significantly large" blighted area and to manage a well-planned, carefully coordinated program designed to revitalize the area and its inhabitants.

THE INTEREST GROUPS INVOLVED

Virtually every urban resident has a stake in housing and urban renewal, and the conflicts and cross-conflicts tend to run deep and be charged with emotion. Business interests are usually concerned with maintaining a viable central business district (CBD) which is accessible, has plenty of parking, is reasonably taxed, and is not surrounded by blight. Yet some businessmen are perfectly willing to abandon the CBD in favor of locations on the outskirts.

In many major urban areas, businessmen have abandoned the central city as a residence, taking their tax dollars with them. Lower income citizens in many instances are the sole surviving inhabitants of the "downtown" area. The main thing that holds them there is poverty. But tradition, the existence of ethnic enclaves, and, in the case of Negroes or Puerto Ricans, the difficulty of "breaking into" the suburbs play a role. Many of these lower income families may not especially like where they live, but they do not want to be uprooted by the bulldozers and forced to move elsewhere, with higher rents, unfamiliar neighbors, and so forth.

Middle-income families have still other interests. They do not want to be squeezed by the high real estate taxes of the city nor overwhelmed by low-income slums. In general, most of them have migrated to the suburbs.

In the midst of these conflicting desires and values stand the real estate interests: developers, contractors, mortgage holders, land-owners, slum lords, the planners and the politicians. The business groups have the strongest possible economic incentives to drive the city and its suburbs in the particular direction which will benefit their properties or activities. The planners, many of them idealists, have a professional interest in seeing that the current conventional wisdom of city planning is brought to reality. The politicians must maintain an economically viable city from a standpoint of revenue and expenditure while continuing to satisfy a majority of the voters.

The net tangible result of the interaction between these groups has, in most cities, been an improved environment for the central business district, prosperity for the suburban communities, and general decay elsewhere.

The federal government's interest is best reflected in the estimated FY 1966 HUD budget (see Table 1).

For many years, the federal government's primary interest has been in selectively stimulating certain types of construction through mortgage insurance. It is still a dominant factor in the mortgage field. Looking at nonfarm 1-4 family dwellings, for example, 35% of the dollar volume of outstanding mortgage debt ($70 billion worth) is FHA insured or VA guaranteed. In addition, in January 1966, the Federal National Mortgage Association's portfolio included $5 billion worth of mortgages obtained through secondary market operations.

Table 1

Estimated FY 1966 HUD Budget

	Amount (000)	Percent
Urban Renewal	$ 688,745	36
College Housing Loans	300,000	15
Low Rent Public Housing	264,405	13
Open Space Land and		
Urban Beautification	235,475	12
Urban Transportation	135,455	7
FNMA	100,000	5
Water and Sewer Facilities	100,000	5
Rehabilitation	41,363	1
Other	122,438	6
	$1,987,881	100%

Since about 1937, the federal government has taken an active interest in the affairs of cities, particularly in slum housing. It has attempted to tread a narrow path, acting as an advisor and provider and leaving the decision to undertake and carry out projects to the municipal governments. Its ability to assume this role gracefully and effectively must inevitably be a key issue for discussion.

THE ISSUES

Given the relatively large amount of experience which certain segments of industry have had with government in the housing and renewal fields, it seems appropriate that we first assess that experience carefully.

First, have the urban priorities favored by businessmen—both those who own CBD property and those who are active in real estate and construction—been well-chosen? Businessmen from both groups have, by and large, elected to undertake those concrete, visible projects which they could accomplish by working with each other—the Penn Centers, the Constitution Plazas, the Golden Triangles, and middle- and higher-income housing projects. Needless to say, not everyone has benefited equally from these projects. As someone evicted by Boston's West End renewal project put it: "It's the old story—the big fish eat the little fish." The plazas and the centers uproot families and neighborhoods, frequently without providing suitable living alternatives. In view of this experience, should business revise its priorities?

Second, have the federal government's objectives been well-chosen? By seeking to encourage local initiative and private enterprise has it neglected its obligation (as a recipient of 70% of all tax revenues) to see that the benefits of federal subsidy are equitably distributed?

Third, given the federal government's objectives, has its strategy been a good one? Has it encouraged businessmen to become actively involved in urban planning and development? Have the incentives been enough and at the right place? Said another way, if you had been spending the government's money, how would you have spent it differently?

These are all questions about the past. Looking ahead, we are confronted by some new issues which arise out of a combination of past experience and a new set of circumstances.

From the past, it was found that wiping out a slum area near the central business district does not necessarily prevent the slum from reappearing elsewhere, sometimes with a dramatic increase in tensions in the new area.

It was found that public housing is not desired by all those who are forced to relocate. It was found that housing is intimately inter-related with education, transportation, and a wide variety of racial and other social problems.

It was found that many of the city's problems are really regional problems which require a regional solution, and that the multitude and autonomy of local governments is a direct impediment to regional action.

This experience poses new problems, most of which are not readily attacked with brick and mortar. To a great extent, they are the traditional problems of government. First, are these valid problems for the businessman to solve? Is he trained and equipped to solve them? Should he be encouraged to try to solve them, and does this mean that he will attempt to impose his values on groups which do not now share them? Or will his own values perhaps change as he gets deeper into the problems?

Second, the federal government has taken a number of steps in response to its experience with cities. It has established new organizations, such as the Office of Economic Opportunity, the President's Crime Commission, and the Department of Housing and Urban Development. It has espoused the doctrine of Creative Federalism, encouraging local initiative with federal assistance and, lately, with federal coordination. The emphasis is on regional planning and on social phenomena. What does the changing federal role mean to you, as a business leader?

(1) Does it mean that the relative position of the state government will be weakened, and hence that your relationship with that government will change?

(2) If the Demonstration Cities Program reaches meaningful proportions, does the influx of federal funds to local officials and agencies mean a weakening of the relative position of business and of its ability to influence the future of the city?

(3) Does the emphasis on the urban region pose a threat to the autonomy of your suburb, particularly to your taxes, your neighborhood, and your children's school?

Third, given the changing nature of the problems and the increased role of the federal government, where will the profit opportunities lie in the future? Will they all be in brick and mortar through government subsidy of one form or another? Or will new markets open up as social changes take place in the slums? Will there be new services which the local government agencies will be requesting of private enterprise? Are the aerospace studies of California's urban problems a step in this direction?

These are not easy questions to answer. It is essential that they be faced prior to formulating any plan of action, however.

POSSIBLE COURSES OF ACTION

Let us assume for the minute that you are a civic-minded business leader with no direct interest in real estate, but with a strong interest in the vitality of the city. There are numerous possibilities open to you. First, you can become directly involved in planning for the future by seeking an elective office or by serving on the board of the local Redevelopment Authority. You can join with other businessmen to form a council or committee which agrees to certain objectives and disciplines itself to accomplish these objectives. Good examples of such groups are San Francisco's Bay Area Council, Pittsburgh's Allegheny Conference, which Mr. John Ryan, President of Mine Safety Appliances Company, will describe in his morning talk, and the Greater Baltimore Committee. One action which such groups frequently take is to establish a revolving development fund to provide financial support for worthy projects.

The Allegheny Conference has gone even further with the establishment of ACTION-Housing, Inc., a private, nonprofit, civic organization. Originally, ACTION-Housing concentrated on middle-income housing. Lately it has responded to the social aspects of urban living through its Neighborhood Urban Extension Program. The use of an organization such as ACTION-Housing to serve as a buffer between the business world and the poor urban neighborhoods should be examined closely. For example, with what group within the poor neighborhood should it work? One Negro leader has said: "The power structure within the Negro community is so complicated that it makes white politics look like child's play." By supporting a middle-income Negro group which is in direct conflict with poorer Negroes, business may be doing more harm than good.

If you are a builder or in the real estate business, you are undoubtedly aware of the variety of federal programs which have been designed to provide you with incentives. There is no need to repeat them here. There are two developments which bear special consideration, however.

The first is the development of entirely new, self-contained communities, near but well outside large urban centers. The advancement of communications and transportation technology has made such cities possible. Reston, Virginia, and Columbia, Maryland, are examples that come to mind. On the more exotic side is the Linear City—extending indefinitely in a straight line and equipped with its own transportation system, shopping centers, job opportunities, and recreation facilities. Is there a future in such new cities and, if so, who will plan them, who will build them, who will finance them, and who will want to live in them?

Second, the proposed Demonstration Cities Program may offer builders a unique opportunity to cooperate on the redevelopment of a large, unified segment of central city land. How should such a redevelopment be organized? Should there be one "systems" contractor reporting to the federal coordinator, and a bevy of sub-contractors? Or should the government serve as the systems contractor, and if it does, what are the implications for the individual builder who must integrate his work with the work of other contractors through a federal coordinator?

SUMMARY

It is not expected that in two hours you will be able to cover all of the issues raised in this brief paper. In all likelihood, as you bring your experience to bear on the problem, additional issues will be generated. Our intention, however, is to have the discussion extend beyond issues. The object of the conference is to develop clearly defined courses of action for you, as business leaders, to consider. You may not reach a consensus as to which course of action is best, but it is hoped that you will go away knowing the implications of each alternative for you, your firm, and your urban area.

Discussion

SOURCES OF GOVERNMENT FRUSTRATION

Most of the government representatives were frustrated by the businessman's lack of concern for the problems of housing and renewal. As might be suspected, this was particularly true of representatives of local government. John Mauro, Director of City Planning in Pittsburgh, put it this way:

My main concern is that, while the business community in Pittsburgh has bought urban renewal as a fact of life and has supported it from its inception, there are quite a few business people throughout the country who look at this as another one of these government subsidy programs where money is being poured down a rat hole and nothing ever emerges. Yet, I don't know of one dollar that is allocated for urban renewal which doesn't wind up ultimately in private hands—whether the recipient works for government, is a contractor, is a lawyer, or whatever. I think all of us in government have failed to translate the effects of renewal on our economy.

Yet rebuilding our communities is an activity which is turned off and on like a faucet. It has no continuity. It's living from hand to mouth, at the whim of the Congress, which is reluctant to fully support and finance these programs because it doesn't have business support continuously.

I can understand a certain antipathy on the part of businessmen to certain social service programs where the taxpayer's money is redistributed to individuals with no visible, tangible short-term payout. But I can't understand why, when most of this money goes into hardware—the very thing that the businesses rely on—why there isn't greater business support of urban renewal and mass transportation.

And, on another occasion while discussing the problem of idle land:

The problem here is that very few of the people in the business community are willing to wait or exercise any patience and understanding when it comes to the major problems of trying to rebuild a city, which may take two or three or four or five generations to rebuild. You get criticism because land lies fallow, or criticism because big chunks of federal money are being appropriated to cities, or criticism because you're relocating people instead of dropping bathrooms down through little holes in the roof to make existing slum structures more habitable. The whole renewal program has been rocked with criticism almost from the date Congress and the federal government entered the picture.

The thing that I can't fathom is why. If the manufacturers today woke up and said that 60% or 70% of our television sets were four years old and obsolete, they would immediately jump in and crank out television sets by the thousands and millions. Or if 40% or 50% of our automobiles were obsolete, all of a sudden we'd have production of automobiles coming out of our ears! And yet the same response doesn't happen in terms of outmoded and obsolete housing or public facilities or schools. We always have had to apologize and pull and strain and try to win public support for expenditures of federal tax dollars that must be invested so that the communities can function for the benefit of our citizens and for private enterprise.

Robert Pease, Director of the Urban Redevelopment Authority in Pittsburgh, was likewise concerned about business apathy, particularly when the contribution of funds served as a substitute for involvement. Speaking of a privately financed renewal program in one city, he commented:

> The Wilmington situation scared me because it could be very good, but it could be very bad. It could be a bunch of businessmen just giving $6 million. It's like giving money to some missionary in Africa to do something, and because you gave, you get the monkey off your back without assuming any responsibility. This we must avoid at all costs.

Sources of Business Frustration

Business frustrations took a variety of forms. Joseph B. McGrath, representing Urban America, Inc., stressed the public policy issues and risks for the future involved in the roundabout approach now employed by the federal government in attempts to provide housing for moderate-to-lower income families:

> I represented the home building industry for about 12 years here in Washington as Director of Governmental Affairs for the National Association of Home Builders. I used to wrestle with the problem of how to get the cost of housing back down to where the average working man can afford either to rent or to buy. The truth of the matter is that builders have done a good job in keeping the basic construction costs relatively stable until just within the last year. This has been done in the face of rising wage rates, which have continuously gone up, and in the face of what I regard as an historical inflation of land in this country. But still there is a gap between what housing costs and what people can pay to live in it. It's widening and the question is: what can we do about it?
>
> In 1961 a basic public policy decision was made in this country, and it may have been in the nature of an interim decision. The public policy decision was that to meet this cost-income gap, especially for lower income families, we will continue to rely on private enterprise, but in a roundabout fashion—with the use of FHA insurance, with the use of money below its market rate, and with the use of the Federal National Mortgage Association to make, in effect, indirect loans of the money. All of this is done

in order to avoid a direct federal loan program such as the programs strongly urged by Senator Lehman, Senator Clark, Senator Douglas, and others in the late 1950s. They said that we should have a middle-income housing program which would consist of direct federal loans, that every builder would be limited to a 5% profit, etc.

Well, that approach was rejected on the ground that the budget simply couldn't afford it. So, to avoid the impact on the budget, the Congress and the Kennedy Administration adopted this indirect route which places a great reliance on the nonprofit organization as the sponsor—to act in the public interest and to help produce the needed housing. If this approach fails over the next six or seven or eight years, then I would think the only other resort to meet this cost-income gap would be direct federal loans for the construction of housing, which will really eliminate a lot of private enterprise, or very greatly restrict it.

Another businessman felt uncomfortable about what his shareholders might think:

Up to now businesses have been hunting for their role either in these nonprofit corporations—we have one in Wilmington, the Greater Wilmington Development Council, which is similar to the Allegheny Conference—or by providing money as seed money for projects through private foundations and things like that. But the major corporations are prevented from building housing, or parking, or transit, or something else, purely because they can't justify this to their stockholders in terms of economic return.

For the most part, however, business concern was centered around the social aspects of housing. Howard Wharton, Acting Commissioner for Urban Renewal, posed the problem:

Urban renewal was never designed to solve all of the social problems. Urban renewal was designed to be a mechanism through which a community could plan a particular redevelopment area, acquire that area, and provide the land so that private investment could build something. By and large this has been very successful in the downtown area—in the rejuvenation areas, in the Pittsburghs, in the Hartfords and in the New Havens—because you have had an interested business investment community that has provided the capital and the buildings and the mechanisms for rebuilding the areas. And while we have had many successful housing projects, the same money and the same investment fraternity and the same mechanisms have not been developed to provide the kinds of large-scale housing that were needed. As a matter of fact, it has only been recently that we have had housing assistance in the middle-income fields, such as 221-d-3,[1] that has provided any mechanism for going into the kind of housing that many of these areas needed and could afford.

So we have this kind of a framework and there are really two types of renewal which have been tried: One fairly successful and one that I think now, along with rehabilitation aids, will become more so. Both of these are extremely important. Certainly the rejuvenation of the downtown in a big city and of the small or middle-sized community in a big town is necessary in order to provide the framework for housing, or better social conditions, or anything else. If this type of effort has been perhaps more obvious and more evident in some of the projects, it's been because it is easier to do.

When you get into the housing and the social aspects, urban renewal itself has probably been more successful in uncovering social problems and bringing them to the forefront and in getting people interested in solutions than it has been in solving them. The only social aid that we could really give in the legislation was relocation assistance. But I think that, as a result of this whole program, and the ferment and the uncovering of these problems, we are now beginning to focus attention on a number of other programs that I hope will bring a greater emphasis to bear on all of this.

There was ample evidence that the social aspects served as a deterrent to business involvement. One investment banker stated this quite directly:

It's the investment banker who is in business to be a middleman between investors and users of capital. Yet, the investment banking industry has had very little interest over the years in the whole field of real estate, in the whole field of housing, and certainly none at all in the field of urban redevelopment. It would seem to me as the years go by that there is something wrong with

---

[1] Shorthand for Section 221-d-3 of the 1961 Housing Act, which relies heavily on low interest rate financing.

this—that the investment banker maybe has talents and avail-ability of funds that somehow under the right conditions should be available for these kinds of purposes.

Secretary Weaver this morning said that the main need was money. I'm not sure that the problem of how you can attract private money to the field of housing and urban development has been given enough thought. Investors in urban real estate keep getting criticized by the politicians as slum lords, and certainly in many cases justifiably so; this kind of stigma doesn't attract investment capital to urban real estate.

John Searles, moderator of the discussion, indicated that his organization—the Metropolitan Development Association in Syracuse—has shied away from the social aspects in the past:

Our objectives lie in four of the five fields which you have been discussing today: transportation, housing and urban renewal, education, and pollution. We have not emphasized the social problem field, although we feel that development problems and people problems are intimately related. Many of our members now feel that groups like ours and the Allegheny Conference can no longer afford the luxury of avoiding the social problems on the grounds that the physical problems are easier to understand and a little bit easier to succeed at. So we are seriously consider-ing whether or not there should be created in our community a related citizen effort to concentrate on the problems of people. I personally hope it will be created.

LOOKING TO THE FUTURE

The representatives of the federal government indicated that the country as a whole was at a critical stage with respect to housing and urban renewal. They suggested that we have learned from past mistakes, that we must face the social aspects squarely, and that the proposed Demonstration Cities Bill marked a turning point in federal policy. Finally, they implored the business community to help.

Robert Wood, Undersecretary of Housing and Urban Develop-ment, began by amplifying the remarks made by Secretary Weaver earlier in the day:

Built into the [Demonstration Cities] approach is a concept that the time has arrived and that it is ripe for specific and meaningful mechanisms for private and public collaboration. Section IV of the Bill is devoted to saying that the city and private sector should mobilize together and participate in a plan which obviously, if we are going to include housing, has to have major private participation.

What lay behind the government's thinking on that legislation was the Allegheny Conference, the Syracuse experiment, and the Wilmington experience, in which I participated some years ago. The notion was that we were beginning to move toward the quasi-public and quasi-private halfway houses and institutions that could take on this whole program together. One of the things we hope for from the cities is real institutional imagination, whether it's a neighborhood corporation, or whether it's a general umbrella organization. This is a way where, by focusing on a specific plan, it is possible to categorize and price out capital investment outlays and social and welfare components. It's that kind of institutional innovation that we are really trying to encourage, and it's that type of specific mechanism that we are looking for.

We look for this, I think, on the fundamental assumption that we have had now a generation of experience in urban renewal, in public housing, and in private housing corporations. It's time to put them together. It's time essentially to combine these resources. We are at a particularly critical time right now and for the next three years. We have caught up, by and large, on the housing supply. We've got about two years before the baby crop of World War II begins to produce babies of their own in new family formations. We're at the point where we've got a set of techniques and know-how that we didn't always have before. Within these next two or three years we'll make the decision about how and where the next building wave goes on. So, this is the other ingredient that I think underscores the intensity of the Secretary's remarks and Mayor Cavanagh's remarks.

Howard [Wharton] and Bob Pease and others here can say far more about the specifics of this, but I did want to underscore the opportunity and the fundamental assumption in the Demonstration Cities Bill—that city hall can't go it alone, and that the federal government can't go it alone.

Howard Wharton continued:

As far as the Demonstration Cities Program is concerned, this is new. I think that this is an extremely important attempt to try to arrive at solutions for neighborhoods and areas which are larger than any we could reach with these isolated programs, although each of these programs—public housing, urban renewal and so on—will be a major component. Whether we have within the present legislation all of the necessary tools and mechanisms, I don't know. But I do know this: Unless we get the legislation, unless we try this, we'll never have an opportunity to find out. This is certainly the most important new legislation yet developed to begin the necessary broad-scale attack on urban problems.

The agency [HUD] now, as you well know, is emphasizing the social approach more heavily, and it's beginning to organize itself in that direction. In the urban renewal programs, we are getting a number of new social tools. This is also true in the other programs. None of this, though, will be accomplished by the federal government alone. It will only be done through the kinds of programs that Bob [Wood] is talking about. It will take the support of business and of all interested community forces—really getting down and finding out what you can do with any of this—before it will be successful.

SUGGESTIONS BY BUSINESSMEN

Businessmen participating in the discussion had a number of suggestions as to why and how business should become involved and how the federal government might help. As to why, Mr. Clark McDonald of the Hardwood Plywood Manufacturers Association pointed to the magnitude of potential business that might be generated, referring, in particular, to an experimental project in New York:

Some of you may not be aware of the enormous amount of business that is available through this New York [rehabilitation] project where they want to remodel 42,000 apartment houses. They are basically the same type of apartment house. They are about five or six stories high; most of them have a 16-inch brick wall; they have one bathroom to a floor.

What they hope to do in New York, and what Mr. Weaver's organization is working on with private industry, is to go into one of these six-story apartment buildings, knock two eight-foot by eight-foot holes in the ceilings all the way down through six floors, strip each apartment down to the bare brick wall, take out the trash through the hole by crane, and then come in with new material through this hole and remodel an entire apartment house in 48 hours. That's the goal, and the idea is that the people who live in these tenement houses will not have to be relocated.

Consider our Washington area. Slum areas were torn down and replaced by beautiful apartments. By the time the beautiful apartments were built most of the people had found new homes, and most of them couldn't afford to move back into the area. In this New York concept, which, I think, if it works, will be used in other cities all over America, they'll keep the people in a hotel for the 48 hours and then move them right back into a brand new, remodeled apartment.

It's a fantastic idea and the amount of building materials that will go into these apartment houses is phenomenal. For example, there'll be four million flush doors or some kind of a panel door going into these apartments. There'll be something like a half-billion feet of some kind of wall paneling. It could be hardwood plywood, it could be paint, it could be wallpaper, it could be gypsum board. But a half-billion feet of some kind of a building material is going to have to cover those brick walls!

Instead of one bathroom to a floor, they are going to put two or four, depending upon the number of apartments on each floor. The way that they are going to close the holes is by bringing in a complete kitchen on one side backed up to a complete bathroom on the other side. They just slip them down in the hole and that will plug the hole and make the bathroom and the kitchen for each apartment on each floor. It's a fantastic, new idea, with new materials and new ways of using the materials.

The Forest Industries Committee is working in this field of re-habilitating housing. I think it's going to generate a terrific amount of business for American industry, and businessmen should be interested in it. U.S. Gypsum, for example, has gone in and bought three of these apartment houses and remodeled them, using their ideas and new methods, because they would like to see U.S. Gypsum products used in the 42,000 apartment houses. Perhaps U.S. Gypsum has a selfish interest, but they still think they are going to break even or make a little profit on the three apartment houses they've bought and remodeled. It is a tremendous project, and what happens in New York City could be duplicated all over America.

As to how businessmen might become involved, a number of possible mechanisms were suggested. The Allegheny Conference, described by Mr. John Ryan earlier in the day, was mentioned again. John Searles described briefly his own organization in Syracuse:

> I work for an association called the Metropolitan Development Association, which is like the Allegheny Conference which Mr. Ryan described this morning. We consist of a hundred businessmen, some of them Harvard Business School graduates, and we differ only in the fact that our mayor and various other representative civic groups are not members. Everybody pays or subscribes to join, and we try to become representative by participating with other groups. We work with the mayor, with our Chamber of Commerce when we can, and with the various other civic groups such as the League of Women Voters, to accomplish a small number of specific objectives. There are about 50 to 125 (depending upon how you classify them) groups like the Allegheny Conference and our own.

Joseph B. McGrath described the use of nonprofit corporations and the role of Urban America, Inc., in establishing such corporations:

> For the past two years, I have been administering a Ford Foundation Grant Program, a major purpose of which is to stimulate the creation of nonprofit development organizations in the country. The organizations are composed primarily of businessmen in the cities where they are created. The purpose is to proliferate the pattern of organization pioneered in Cleveland and Pittsburgh. You heard this morning about the Pittsburgh Housing Development Fund. There are others in the country.
> The Ford Foundation Grant Program that I am administering for Urban America stems from an initial study, also funded by the Ford Foundation. It was an analysis of private development funds, done by two experts from Pittsburgh, entitled: *Selected Characteristics of Private Development Funds*. The report analyzed twelve funds in ten different cities. All of the funds were

organized efforts on the part of businessmen to do something about the environment in which they found their businesses placed and about the people who were working for them.

In the last two years, I have had some of the most interesting, timely, and I think hopeful experiences of my career in dealing with leading businessmen in a number of cities throughout the United States. These include the cities of Hartford, Cambridge, Baltimore, Phoenix and Washington, D. C., plus some other places, including New York City. In each one of these cities I have been meeting with key business leaders. They are concerned, for their own reasons, about the housing conditions in their cities and are determined to do something about it. We are supplied with the funds to help them. In short, we can spend our Ford Foundation money to assist them in the creation of a private nonprofit development organization.

I am happy to say that three or four of these have already been created. Let me cite to you some examples. In Hartford, the very same businessmen who put together the Hartford Constitution Plaza, one of the outstanding downtown urban renewal projects in the country, have now formed the Greater Hartford Housing Development Corporation. It is a private, nonprofit development fund whose purpose is to initiate housing projects. It is not designed to compete with private enterprise. It is to initiate projects in the moderate-to-lower income field that are badly needed by the city. These projects are needed by the Negro families in the city, and they are needed by other people in the city. The leader there has been Mr. Roger Wilkins, a senior vice president of the Travelers Life Insurance Company. Senior vice presidents of the other life insurance companies are also on the organizing committee, together with the major bankers and the publisher of one of Hartford's newspapers.

In Cambridge, Massachusetts, the leading business, university and civic leaders have already formed The Cambridge Corporation, with our assistance. Really, they have put together a "third force" in the city of Cambridge—a city with which I think all of you are familiar. This is a new, private, nonprofit development corporation with one objective: to improve the housing conditions in the city of Cambridge. We supplied a basic study to assist them in their thinking. We have supplied other funds to help them. We helped to locate the executive director who has been hired by the

Cambridge Corporation. Dr. Killian, the Chairman of MIT's Board, is the chairman of the board of trustees. Dr. Pusey, the President of Harvard, is on the board. General Gavin, Charles Coolidge and other well-known Boston and Cambridge civic leaders are also on the board. Both Harvard and MIT have agreed to put up $250,000 each on a matching basis. The corporation would like to have a total of about a million dollars raised: $500,000 from the universities and $500,000 from other sources, especially business sources. The president of the Chamber of Commerce for Cambridge is a vital part of this prospective fund raising.

In the city of Washington, D. C., and in the city of Baltimore we are dealing with other business leaders. The Greater Baltimore Committee, for example, which is primarily responsible for the Charles Center downtown development, has now turned its attention to housing. They will put together a private development organization to initiate projects which otherwise would not take place in Baltimore. Mr. Robert Levi, who is president of the Hecht Company department stores, James Rouse, the mortgage banker and creator of the new town at Columbia, Maryland, and other businessmen whom some of you would know are the instigators in this effort in Baltimore.

In Corning, New York, the Ingersoll-Rand and Corning Glass Companies have decided that they must do something about the condition of housing and in fact about the general environment, in the city of Corning. They have great expansion plans and this matter of housing really means something to them in terms of employee and executive recruitment and retention. They formed a private development corporation. They got commitments for an initial $100,000 just to get the thing going. They are in the process of hiring an executive director and they have located the land they want to start developing on. It will all be done through the mechanism of a nonprofit development organization. And the mainspring for it all is the farseeing and alert business support, coming in large part from the senior executives and officers of the Corning Glass Works Company.

There are other cities that I could tell you about, but let me finish by reciting to you an experience which just happened to me. I was invited to go to the city of Rochester as a guest of the Urban League. The National Committee Against Discrimination in Housing has been in Rochester working with the business community and civic leadership, and they convinced the businessmen that something must be done about the housing conditions in Rochester. So the businessmen said, "We're with you. We agree with you. But what do we do? How do we translate what we think ought to be done in the city into some action? Where do we seize the initiative?"

The answer from the NCADH was: "Get ahold of Urban America and ask Joe McGrath up here. Let him tell you about his Ford Foundation program and the new nonprofit development technique you could use." I went up, and we met around a table with no publicity whatsoever. A senior vice president of Eastman Kodak was there, as were the executive vice president of Xerox, the heads of some of the banks, of the department stores and others.

The key men were there and we talked about one thing: creating a new permanent financing vehicle in Rochester with which they could initiate some things in the field of housing they felt should be done. There was a real desire to seize the initiative and move. And given a chance, I really think they will do it because the supply of money and leadership is present in Rochester, as it is in Hartford, as it is in Cambridge, and as it is in Corning. Without the leadership and a supply of money to initiate things, you can't get moving. But with them both, and with the cooperation of the city officials, there is indeed a lot that can be done by a determined business community.

Willian Van Meter described the activities of the United States Chamber of Commerce:

MR. VAN METER: Mr. Chairman, as a representative of the Chamber of Commerce of the United States I was, of course, delighted to hear reference to the work of local chambers. I've been thinking about the question you posed initially, and some of the other speakers have posed it, namely—what can businessmen do? It occurred to me that a very significant comment was made this morning on several occasions. I recall principally the one by Mayor Cavanagh when he said that local problems must be solved locally. He also made the significant comment that there are far broader problems of a social nature. I don't think we can divorce these problems in any consideration of urban renewal.

Let me make several comments that in turn might be suggestive to this group. We have operated under the belief that, in order to harness the business strength to meet the problems of urban renewal—and we are staunchly for this—you need organization. We are not wedded to any particular type. You have your development associations. You have all sorts of organizations which can do this. On the other hand, we have found that by actively promoting a technique with our membership, which by and large are the local chambers of commerce throughout the country, we can, in many instances, encourage them to create the mechanisms through which the businessmen can be active in urban problems.

We have knowledge that some 400 communities have indeed embarked on a program which is designed not only to focus on urban renewal, but also to meet the problems of total community development in all of its aspects. We have high hopes that this will be productive. We are pursuing this very vigorously. I think Mr. McGrath probably is aware of some of the things that we have done. We are endeavoring to stimulate and motivate local business leaders in their communities to play their rightful role in participating in these projects. I suggest that this is a mechanism in existence that can be harnessed with leadership to the job at hand.

BUSINESSMAN: I might say that the local chambers are quite a bit ahead of the national chamber in this quarter.

MODERATOR: It is sort of interesting that you comment this way. It has seemed to some of us who are battling it out at the local level that some of the legislation that would be very helpful has been opposed by the National Chamber and supported by the local chambers. I wonder what causes that difference?

MR. VAN METER: Well, it is for the local chambers to decide their own position. The local chambers themselves decide our positions. We don't decide them here.

MODERATOR: Well, there have been various groups that have visited communities and have talked about opposing the urban renewal legislation and opposing the Housing Act of 1965.

MR. VAN METER: I suggest that you examine the record of the last twelve months as to the attitude of the National Chamber on this issue. It will surprise you.

All of the approaches described above are direct approaches. They involve the direct participation of business groups. A number of indirect approaches were also suggested. A typical example was described by one businessman:

You've got in existence a number of organizations that I think the business community could get behind. Take the churches. Whether you like it or not, the federal government has available substantial sums of money which it can use to give 100% loans with 3% interest for a 40-year period. First you have to digest the fact that maybe 3% money is wrong, or sinful, or socialistic. You have to get that out of your craw. But once you've overcome that hurdle, you can start talking the way McDonald[2] talks; in terms of the number of bathtubs, or the number of bricks, or the number of yards of concrete, or the number of square feet of flooring. Don't even think of it in terms of the social need. Simply think of it in terms of obsolescence. Think of it purely in terms of business.

For example, I am a consultant to the Bridgeport Council of Churches. This is a group of 90 churches in Bridgeport that have been trying for five years to put together a housing-for-the-elderly project. We got them a $6,285,000 commitment from FHA. They almost lost it because they lacked $10,000 at one time. I would have lost a beautiful fee and the landowner would have lost a sale. He would have had to take back 10 acres of ground and there wouldn't have been that good a use available for a long time to come. I wouldn't even want to calculate the number of jobs involved in building $6,285,000 worth of housing—340 units. Five years of work and energy of the finest people in Bridgeport would have gone right down the drain.

I think that this is the kind of thing that we can do. We can provide some seed capital—some floating money. I think a $25,000 loan to this group—to the Bridgeport Council of Churches —five years ago would have enabled them to finish their project in probably three years. It could have been paid back out of the proceeds of the mortgage loan and made available to another group.

Finally Robert Pease, Executive Director of Pittsburgh's Urban Redevelopment Authority described the unusual and potentially fruitful approach which his agency is using in Pittsburgh's Hill District. He stated the need for a "total community commitment" on the part of businessmen to such a program:

We spend a great deal of time in the slum. I was intrigued by Bob Wood's use of the phrase "halfway house." A halfway house

[2] See p. 65.

in the Hill District of Pittsburgh is a delivery station for dope. So, when you use a term, you've got to be careful where you're using it, because it means one thing in a church and something else somewhere else.

We talked to housewives, and we talked to operators of "half-way houses," and gamblers, and numbers writers and so on. We found something quite interesting—interesting to me because I was educating myself in this process. We found that these folks had a varied awareness of the need for improving the environment —for improving the housing. They had a vague desire for the kids to finish school, and so on. But they really weren't equipped to cope with the longer-run kinds of problems.

Basically, these are decent people. Keep that in mind. They are also people with a very valid system of values. Keep that in mind too.

The things that kept repeating all the time, as we talked to the people—from the racketeers to the housewives—were four things, in this order of priority: garbage pickup, street repairs, street lights, and recreation. There are 3,500 kids in this little area between the ages of five and twelve, and no real playground in the place for them.

The people were concerned with the immediate problems, you see. So we set about to solve the immediate problems. The mayor supported us and the council members at City Hall supported us. A street cleaning program was adopted. Garbage pickup programs were adopted. And we arrested some of the people who were throwing garbage out on the Hill. And things were better. We improved 12 streets. We put up street lights when and where the people asked for them. We built them new blockrooms. We cleared off some lots, and what have you.

Amazingly, the results have been this: the people now are meeting with us every other Thursday night, in the heart of this area, at various locations. They now have adopted short-range goals and long-range goals which begin to deal with things like housing and things like integration—not Negroes moving someplace else but whites moving in, if it can be made good enough.

What's happening here is that we're developing a concept with the people involved—a communication between this area and City Hall—with City Hall and the community responding to a hope that's developing.

There is one thing that scared me about Bob Weaver's remarks this morning. Bob Weaver stated, and I wish I could quote it more accurately, that this Demonstration Cities thing is going to develop a great promise and a great hope for the people in these ghetto areas of the city. And yet on the other hand, he turned around and said there's not enough money to really do it.

Take New York City. New York City is a national problem, not a New York City problem. Mayor Lindsay will never solve the problem of New York by himself. There are three great slum areas in New York—Bedford-Stuyvesant, South Bronx, and Harlem. There are others, to be sure, but these are the three great concentrations. In these areas, in substandard housing, live about 1,300,000 people. In Central and East Harlem alone live about 336,000 people.

The Demonstration Cities Program, as it was proposed before Congress, will not solve the problem of Harlem. And yet, if the problem of Harlem isn't solved, what hope do we have of solving all the little Harlems throughout the United States? This is the question I was raising my hand frantically to ask when Mr. Weaver was cut off this morning.

I think the real hope might come from the businessmen in this country not necessarily giving money, even though money's important, and I've never denied that money's important. But in addition, they must develop what I like to call a "total community commitment" to these areas.

Mr. Pease went on to describe how $10,000 worth of business support has gone a long way within the structure of a program such as the one in the Hill District:

In this slum area of Pittsburgh [the Hill District] we've developed an Urban Youth Action Program. With $10,000 of private money—which is very little—we have developed a program in which 8th-grade through 12th-grade kids work for four hours on a Saturday at a buck and a quarter an hour, and 6th- through 8th-grade kids work for three hours on a Saturday for a dollar an hour. These kids have to meet three criteria: (1) they need parental permission, (2) they have to be in school—we're not interested in school dropouts for this program, and (3) they have to attend training sessions. Work assignments are made by five children who work more than just on Saturdays.

These kids—twenty-two of them each Saturday—now work in their own neighborhood to clear off lots. They work in drug stores.

They work in doctor's offices. They work wherever these five kids assign them to work. And we, the Renewal Authority, pay them.

This little tiny effort with this small group of kids has now put us in direct contact with 700 boys and girls in this district and has put us, more fruitfully, in direct contact with their parents. And this has caused so much excitement in the city of Pittsburgh that the city is now giving $100,000 to multiply the program tenfold. So, hopefully, we can work 200 kids each Saturday.

These kids have the greatest spirit, the greatest enthusiasm, and the greatest intellect I've ever seen. It's a moving experience to see the responsibility these kids are willing to assume in making their own neighborhood a better place to live.

I think that rather than getting so complicated and off in the wild blue yonder in social problems and Demonstration Cities problems and so on, we need to lower ourselves—if you consider it lowering—to deal with these very basic, immediate problems like cleaning off a vacant lot or like making a contribution to this South Street neighborhood.

Out of this is coming, in the power structure of Pittsburgh, in the governmental structure of Pittsburgh, and in the ghetto itself, a unique and an important understanding and communication about the problems in that area. I think we've got a lion by the tail, and we're not going to let go. Out of this may come a program which is more meaningful than anything that's been devised since we've had programs.

A few businessmen offered suggestions directly to the federal government as to how greater business involvement might be stimulated. One suggestion was a tax incentive:

I think there is one means whereby private capital—and not so much through the investment route as through major businesses— could be induced to invest more in the cities. This is through tax incentives. We've seen it used to encourage private capital investment through the 7% tax credit. Conceivably something along the same lines could be used for corporations who are making some kind of major urban investments in their communities.

Another businessman who is close to the housing industry had a somewhat more radical suggestion:

I don't know whether we are facing the problem squarely. Suppose we were sitting here saying that there are a lot of people in this country who can't afford to buy new cars and yet who shouldn't be driving ten-year-old junks. If we know that a new car costs $2,500 and that they can't afford it, how are we going to get them a new car for $500? This seems to me somewhat comparable to what we are saying about housing, and this is why there are so many problems.

In response we have invented devices that help to make up the difference. We use nonprofit corporations; we use lower interest rates; we experiment with all kinds of things to try to monkey the basic fact that you can't afford, with today's cost of materials and labor, to build a new place to house a family which is in the income bracket you're concerned about.

One of the things we're overlooking is depreciation and obsolescence. So perhaps we should be more honest about what you can build and what price you can build it at. If we got busy and built some good housing, in the course of ten years it would depreciate enough so that some of it would then be rentable at the price that people with lower incomes can afford to pay.

SUMMARY

Many of the comments by businessmen reflect their past frustrations. The lack of incentives, the unpleasantness of coping with social problems, and the maze of "roundabout" government programs have been major deterrents to involvement.

The government representatives seemed to suggest: (1) that they are aware of past difficulties; (2) that things are under way which could radically change the nature of housing and renewal programs, and (3) that business help will be needed badly to bring these changes about. Attention was focused on the proposed Demonstration Cities Bill, although Robert Pease's description of his activities in Pittsburgh suggests that things are changing at the local level as well.

It was not at all clear that the mechanisms used by businessmen are designed to take maximum advantage of the new thrust in governmental activity. They are mechanisms designed principally to finance and construct buildings. Clearly, the government programs assume, perhaps for the first time, that housing is, at its root, a social problem, and that government programs must treat it as such.

Thus, perhaps the most significant challenge posed by the discussion was the challenge to business to design mechanisms which will view housing and urban renewal as social problems and which will treat them as such. This raises the issue of whether business should become involved in the solution of social problems. That issue was not resolved.

Selected Bibliography

Abrams, Charles. *Man's Struggle for Shelter in an Urbanizing World* (Cambridge: MIT, 1964).

Chinitz, Benjamin. *City and Suburb: The Economics of Metropolitan Growth* (Englewood Cliffs, N.J.: Prentice-Hall, 1960).

Jacobs, Jane. *Death and Life of Great American Cities* (New York: Random House, 1961).

Vernon, Raymond. *Myth and Reality of our Urban Problems, The Stafford Little Lectures of 1961 with Seminar Discussion* (Cambridge: Joint Center for Urban Studies, 1962).

Wilson, James Q. *Urban Renewal* (Cambridge: MIT, 1966).

APPENDIX IV-A

Questions and Answers to Explain the Demonstration Cities Act of 1966[a]

What is a comprehensive city demonstration program?

It is a program to improve large slum and blighted sections by use of all available federal aids and local private and public resources to improve the general welfare of people who live and work in the areas.

What is required to have a demonstration program?

There are eight requirements to obtain this federal assistance.

(1) The local program must be large in scope, both physically and socially. It should aim at wiping out or arresting blight and decay in entire sections or neighborhoods. It should increase the supply of decent housing at low and moderate cost. It should make marked progress toward improving the education and reducing disease and idleness of those who live in slums and blighted areas. And it should have a sound impact on the entire city.

(2) The program must contribute to a well-balanced city. One result must be adequate city-wide facilities. This would include better schools, transportation and recreation, good access to centers of employment, and housing for all income levels.

(3) The program must call for widespread citizen participation in all its phases. It should provide jobs and training for those living in the area, as well as offer social and educational services to the poor and disadvantaged living there.

(4) The program must be assured of enough local resources to reach completion on schedule.

(5) The program must be supported by all local government units concerned. Local agencies to be involved must show their intent to cooperate with the city government so that the program will be carried out with complete coordination.

(6) The program must assure that those displaced by renewal efforts will be satisfactorily relocated.

(7) The program will assure full opportunity in choice of housing for all citizens.

(8) The program will meet such other requirements as the Secretary shall call for to carry out the purposes of the Act.

---

[a] A publication of the department of Housing and Urban Development dated April 18, 1966.

What other factors must be considered?

The Secretary must make five added judgments in determining whether the program should be approved for a city. They are:

(1) He must make sure that local laws and other local requirements are consistent with program goals.

(2) He must be certain that the program will apply high standards of design and not destroy existing natural, historical or cultural characteristics.

(3) He must decide that costs are held down by use of the best building methods, materials and design.

(4) He must make sure that the program will reduce housing segregation by race and income levels.

(5) He must see to it that the program fits in well with comprehensive planning for the entire metropolitan or urban area.

What amount of federal aid can the city get for planning the program?

The Secretary can pay the city's demonstration agency 90% of the costs of planning and developing the program.

After program approval, what amount of federal aid can be obtained?

Grants will be available to meet 80% of the costs of administering the program. In addition, a grant up to 80% of the required local share of the cost of projects or activities assisted by federal grants-in-aid will be available to help carry out all the projects or activities included as part of the program. There are safeguards to assure that a city cannot take advantage of this federal aid program by cutting down on its level of expenditures on activities similar to those assisted in the demonstration program.

Will the federal government help with program direction?

Yes, by establishing an Office of the Federal Coordinator. The Director of this office will make every effort to achieve the most effective coordination of federal grant-in-aid programs undertaken in connection with the demonstration programs. Also, the Secretary will provide technical assistance to help cities plan, develop and administer the demonstration programs.

Will other federal agencies cooperate?

Yes. The Act requires the Secretary to consult with other federal departments and agencies on all aspects involving federal grant-in-aid programs. He will do this before making a commitment for grants for city demonstration programs.

CHAPTER V

Urban Transportation

The discussion on urban transportation illustrates, perhaps more vividly than any of the other discussions, one very significant theme of the conference. In the absence of a crisis, it is unlikely that any individual or group in a city will look beyond its immediate, short-term interests in its response to an urban problem. Perhaps the easiest way to illustrate this theme is to present the issues suggested for discussion—as put forth in the background paper and by John Kohl, the moderator—and then to examine the response of various interested parties to these issues.

Background Paper

The provision of adequate transportation facilities poses one of the most perplexing problems faced by any urban area. It is difficult to predict future transportation needs. It is difficult to obtain any kind of agreement on a transportation proposal, particularly when it is a regional rather than a local proposal. Given this lack of agreement and given the fact that different interest groups perceive one form of transportation as more beneficial than another, it is difficult to finance any large-scale improvement in mass transit. Yet urban transportation is the key to the vitality of the urban area as a whole, and it may be essential to the survival of the central city. The May 20 discussion on transportation will focus on what the businessman can do to improve the movement of people into and within his city. As preparation for that discussion, this paper will first provide some background information. It will then identify the interest groups involved in urban transportation decision-making, and will suggest some issues which arise out of the sometimes conflicting interests of these groups. Finally, it will offer some possible alternative courses of action which might be evaluated and augmented as the discussion proceeds.

INTRODUCTION

Urban transportation was originally supported by real estate speculators and power companies. The speculators needed a way to get people to newly developed land and the power companies found electric railways to be good customers or subsidiaries. The electric railways prospered until the advent of the automobile in the 1920s, and then began to falter. The automobile offered privacy, speed, flexibility, stature, and pride of ownership. The "Toonerville Trolley" was no match for the car.

Automobiles and roads have dominated the scene ever since. The 1960 census reveals the following distribution of work trips by mode of transportation:

	Private Autos	Public Trans- portation	Walk and Miscel- laneous
New York	31%	55%	14%
Other cities with over 500,000 population	69%	17%	14%
Cities with less than 500,000 population	74%	8%	18%

The automobile has, at best, been a mixed blessing for the city. A car is a bulky item, particularly when, on the average, only 1.6 people ride in it. Very few highways are large enough not to be bogged down to a standstill during rush hour, frustrating everyone on them. There is thus a constant demand by commuters for wider expressways, which chew up tax-free land at a rapid clip, and for more parking lots, which usurp building sites. There is often resistance by citizens and businesses who will be uprooted by the new roads. The freeway program has forced more residential relocations than any other public construction program in the United States. More cars mean more expensive traffic-control systems and more police to apprehend violators, all of which appear in the city budget. Cars produce exhaust, and in many cities this has meant a dramatic rise in air pollution.

To many urban leaders, a further increase in the use of the automobile is intolerable. Looking around for alternatives, however, they confront the image which has come to dominate mass transit: slow, inconvenient, hot, dirty, and crowded with all classes of people. To change the image usually means to invest in new equipment, to lay out new routes, and to shift from a production orientation to a marketing orientation within the transit company. That is a lot to expect of an entrenched organization, be it public or private. In addition, if federal funds are to be used in the process, all the different factions must get together and come up with an acceptable regional plan. To see how difficult this might be, we need only look at the interest groups involved.

THE INTEREST GROUPS

Nonbusiness Groups

To the uninitiated, the number and variety of groups which have an interest in urban transportation is startling. Let us start with the nonbusiness groups, specifically those within the central city government. First, there is the mayor's office, the manager, or the city council, and sometimes all three. They must be responsive to the voting public, and hence responsive to those who wish to avoid relocation, high taxes, segregation, et cetera. There is usually an Office of City Planning which is responsive to the mayor or manager. Slightly more autonomous are the professionally run agencies in the central city: the redevelopment authority, the highway department, the parking authority, the port authority (if appropriate) and, usually, the transit authority. Most major transit companies are owned, or are about to be owned, by public agencies, the Washington, D.C. system being a notable exception.

In contrast to the large, central city government organization is a multiplicity of small urban governments surrounding the central city. Under the basic principles of home rule, each has its prerogatives. Unless the suburban public officials yield to some kind of regional government, such as a county government or a special transit district, the task of extending rights-of-way out from the central city can be an insurmountable one.

State governments usually play two key roles. First, most of the highway funds, and the interstate funds in particular, go through the state highway departments. Second, in many states the state legislature must pass enabling legislation for the establishment of local agencies to cope with transit problems. Just recently, two states—Massachusetts and Pennsylvania—have provided state aid on a limited basis.

Interest in urban transportation at the federal level was meager until about 1955. Again, the home rule philosophy dominated. Since the middle 1950s, however, two federal departments have been active and have sought Congressional support for urban transit systems. The Commerce Department, through the Bureau of Public Roads, looks after the 41,000 mile interstate expressway system set up in the 1956 Federal Aid Highway Act. Forty-five per cent of the $41 billion cost of the interstate network will be for urban expressways, raising their total mileage from 2,875 (in 1960) to 9,200 miles by 1971. Commerce also engages in research projects which affect urban transportation, the Boston-Washington Corridor Project being a notable example.

When the Housing and Home Finance Agency was merged into HUD, it maintained responsibility for administering grants under the Urban Mass Transportation Act of 1964. The bulk of the $375 million provided by the act was to be for matching capital grants on a 2/3-1/3 basis. Approximately $30 million, however, was earmarked for research and demonstration grants.

In addition to all of the interested government bodies, there are two noteworthy nonbusiness, nongovernment interest groups which deserve attention. The first is labor. With from 60% to 70% of all mass transit expenses going to labor, it is reasonable to expect labor to be vitally concerned. It is not surprising to find a number of labor-protecting clauses in the 1964 Urban Mass Transportation Act. Second, we cannot ignore the groups of citizens who may be directly affected by any particular project. In Boston, for example, local citizens' groups have held up an inner belt project for almost a decade.

Business Groups

Business is not a unified force in urban transportation. The businessmen in the central business district of any urban area are usually an identifiable group. They want better highways, better parking facilities, and better mass transit radiating out of the central city so that they, their employees, and their customers can commute easily to and from the CBD. The suburban businessmen form another group. They are indifferent to the rush-hour traffic problem in the central city. In fact, they may view it as an advantage in that it tends to protect their investment in the suburb by keeping workers and shoppers out of the downtown area.

Cutting across these two groups are specific organizations with special interests. Local chambers of commerce, according to a disputed survey made by the United States Chamber, are opposed to federal aid of any kind on the grounds that it will usurp local powers. There are, however, some notable exceptions to this finding if, in fact, it is true at all.

Most commuter railroads would, by and large, like nothing better than to get out of the urban transit business. But given that they are in it by franchise, they want to be assured of federal aid, and they want to protect themselves against encroachment by other local mass transit companies. Finally, it is not surprising to find the auto manufacturers supporting highways, and the companies who manufacture rapid transit equipment supporting rapid transit (WABCO in Pittsburgh, for example), and so forth.

It should not be concluded from this enumeration of interest groups that each group is unalterably opposed to, or in conflict with, the others. In fact, as federal involvement in urban transportation increases, and as the survival of the city becomes an issue, strange bedfellows are found at the local level. A toll bridge will help finance a rapid rail system. A chamber of commerce will recommend that a federal grant be obtained for a specific purpose. Self-interest, after all, is only in the eyes of the perceiver, and as the world changes, so must the perception.

THE ISSUES

Out of the interplay between interest groups arises a number of issues which must be resolved, or at least articulated, before meaningful action can take place.

First, there is the relationship of transportation to the urban area as a whole, particularly with regard to land use and the relative significance of the CBD. Back in the nineteenth century, it was clear that urban transportation networks were constructed to facilitate land development. Now it is not at all clear whether land use determines the transportation system or vice versa. Three particular issues highlight the complexity of this relationship:

(1) Should a public investment be made in rapid transit which radiates out from the central business district when such an investment may undermine existing, not to mention future, private investment in suburban communities?

(2) Should a central city resident be heavily taxed to provide transit facilities which enable suburban residents to live in a suburban community and avoid city property taxes?

(3) In the interest of promoting rapid transit and luring commuters away from their automobiles, should a public transit company be allowed to operate predominantly express service from the suburbs to the central business district, when such a service encourages segregation of minority groups in the "grey" areas through which the express car speeds?

Second, there is the issue of public vs. private ownership of local transit companies. While advocates of private ownership have clearly been losing ground, they point to superior efficiency (as measured by operating ratios) of the few remaining private companies. They credit the profit motive and the private, politically independent business executive with such performance. The advocates of public ownership counter that the private owner is not sensitive to the "social obligations" of local transit, and that the private company is constantly embroiled in labor disputes and in court action over regulatory matters. The public ownership advocates may be winning, but the issue is certainly not a closed one. What, for example, is the future of a public authority (with control over both transportation and parking) which contracts out to private companies many of the transit operations?

The public vs. private ownership discussion raises a third issue which lies at the heart of any transportation decision. How is a transportation system to be evaluated? Do you examine some measure of efficiency of each of its parts, in much the same way you might look at a profit center? If so, what measure should be used? Is it cost/seat mile, or profit, or operating efficiency of equipment, or number of passengers transported, or ability to solve the peak problem, or what? Some have argued that it makes no sense to examine each part, but only to look at the whole system as a system to see if it serves the functions it should serve for the entire region. The transit operating executive tends to view this suggestion with horror, pointing out that, in practice, it would undermine the whole concept of accountability. There would be no way to evaluate an individual supervisor in charge of one of the elements of the system. The advocate of a "functional" approach responds that it is the accounting system, not the functional concept, which is at fault. To him, it makes little difference whether one part of the system operates inefficiently or at a loss, as long as there is a net gain to the community as a whole. The "functional" approach has been gaining ground lately, as reflected in a number of large transportation studies in Detroit, Chicago, Pennsylvania, New Jersey, and New York. Its implications for local interest groups should be examined carefully. What constitutes a "net gain for the community as a whole," for example, and to what extent should a conscious decision to expand the role of the central city (as in Philadelphia) or to improve the CBD while encouraging major satellite centers (as in Detroit) be allowed to dominate plans for constructing or improving transportation facilities in the entire area?

During any evaluation, one particular issue will inevitably come up: what technology or blend of technologies should be used? The rail advocates claim that if workers who commute to and from a central city during the rush hours are concentrated along corridors, the high capacity and low variable operating costs per passenger of the rail system give it a distinct advantage despite the high fixed costs of constructing and maintaining stations and rights-of-way. Those favoring bus systems are quick to point out that except for a few large cities, New York being the prime example, such concentrations of commuters do not exist, and that the flexibility of the bus makes it the logical choice for most cities and a necessary ingredient in any city. Finally, of course, the groups favoring automobiles insist that commuters prefer the privacy and comfort of their own car, and that roads and parking lots should be stressed.

Over time, the arguments among these groups has bordered on the emotional. As a result, the claims of each group have tended to be made in generalities, sometimes ignoring the extremely situational nature of any transportation analysis. To overcome this difficulty, we must ask: What mix of technologies makes the most sense for a particular city with a particular geography at a particular point in time? Looking ahead, how should newly developing technologies—monorails, hydrofoils, ground-effect machines, et cetera—be incorporated into present decisions regarding the sequential improvement of transit facilities over time. Third, to what extent will automation affect labor costs and hence the tradeoffs between technologies?

The increase of federal activity in the urban transportation business raises a whole range of issues. At one extreme, one might ask if a federal government with "perfect" planning capabilities should have the option of imposing its findings on a local community. There are strong historical precedents against any such imposition. If it is claimed that the federal government is not imposing its findings but merely aiding the local community, a careful look at how this is done seems called for. At one level, the federal government assists cities in making large studies such as those mentioned in the preceding paragraph. At another level, the federal government can require an acceptable regional plan before allocating any funds for hardware. While this has not been a significant issue to date, it could become one as programs such as the Demonstration Cities Program gain momentum. If federal approval of plans does become significant, what criteria is the government going to use in determining the city's problems and arriving at acceptable solutions? In particular, what groups does it consult in reaching its conclusions? Does increased federal planning and support activity mean that different people will be making transportation decisions guided by different pressure groups with different interests?

At a minimum, these five issues must be faced prior to formulating any plan of action.

ALTERNATIVE COURSES OF ACTION

Objectives

From the preceding description of the urban transportation problem, it should be clear that what business will wish to accomplish will depend quite heavily on what kind of business we are talking of and what kind of a city is involved.

Civic-minded business leaders (assuming they are not equipment suppliers or transit operators) will probably be concerned with the city as a whole, particularly with the relationship between the central city and the suburbs. The suburban businessman may well want to maintain a central city, but is not likely to be concerned with the rush-hour commuting problem. He is interested in the central city primarily for the business services, culture, or sports which it offers.

Given his particular interests, what the businessman can accomplish may be heavily constrained by the city in which he lives. If it is a new community, such as Phoenix, the car can dominate without much difficulty. If it is an old, established city, obtaining new rights-of-way may be extremely difficult and expensive, and primary attention may have to be focused on improving the existing modes of transit. If the city lies in the middle ground, there is room to work toward the transportation expert's dream of a "balanced system."

Organization of Effort

In rare cases, the businessman may be able to act as an independent agent by assuming a public office and pushing his own interests. His company can perhaps act independently by financing a transportation study or a demonstration. But in most instances, if he is to have a significant effect on the transportation system, the businessman must act jointly with others who share his interests. Limited experience with joint action in cities to date bears this out. In San Francisco, for example, we find the San Francisco Bay Area Council, founded and supported by a group of business leaders, pushing hard for a new rail rapid transit system for the Bay Area. Working closely with government groups, they got voters to approve a bond issue, got the government to help finance a demonstration, and were instrumental in establishing the now-famous Bay Area Rapid Transit District to undertake construction of the project. Citing another example, Washington's Downtown Committee is considered by many to have been instrumental in inaugurating the Minibus service in downtown Washington.

On the other side, there is some evidence to support the conjecture that a lack of unity on the part of business leaders can be fatal to an improvement in transit facilities. It has been said, for example, that one of the factors contributing to the defeat of the downtown distribution subway in Cleveland was the disagreement within the central business district retail community over the location of the subway.

If he chooses to act jointly with others, there are a number of basic questions which the businessman must resolve. First, who is going to be in the group? If it is not business leaders, what is to be the source of the group's influence? Second, how will the group maintain group discipline when self-interests do not always coincide? Third, as an individual or a company, he must determine carefully what he is giving up to join a group and assess whether the gains exceed the losses.

Financing

The financing of any urban transit project will vary widely, depending on: (1) the type of project; (2) the stage of the project; (3) belief in federal support; and (4) the cohesiveness of local interest groups. Looking at the San Francisco project as a thoroughly planned, rapid rail system with cohesive support and no qualms about federal support, we have the following financial breakdown:

General Obligation Bond Issue	$794 million
California State Toll Bridge Authority Revenue Bonds	133 million
District Revenue Bonds	71 million
Federal Funds	8 million

The project's costs are already exceeding its estimates and it will be interesting to note whence the additional funding will come.

If the project is a highway project, there are a great number of possibilities. It may still be possible, for example, to influence the routing of the present Interstate System. If present Interstate plans are firm, now is an opportune time to consider the future of the Interstate System. It has been proposed that Interstate construction be extended well into the 1970s presumably with the federal government continuing to cover 90% of the cost.

If the project cannot wait for a new Interstate Act, there is the well-established Primary and Secondary Road Program, with 50% federal and 50% state funding available. In addition, city, county, and state governments will finance local access roads.

Parking can also be handled in a variety of ways. One possibility is to design parking facilities into urban renewal plans, and take advantage of land write-downs to make a private facility feasible. Another is to persuade local authorities that public parking areas are in the best long-run interest of the city despite the immediate loss of taxes which would result.

These are merely a few suggestions. Presumably others will be proposed as the discussion develops.

SUMMARY

It is not expected that in two hours you will be able to cover all of the issues raised in this brief paper. In all likelihood, as you bring your experience to bear on the problem, additional issues will be generated. The discussion is being structured, however, to extend beyond issues. The object of the conference is to develop clearly defined courses of action for you, as business leaders, to consider. You may not reach a consensus as to which course of action is best, but it is hoped that you will go away knowing the implications of each alternative for you, your firm, and your urban area.

Discussion

INTRODUCTORY REMARKS BY JOHN KOHL

We have a rather large assignment this afternoon—the general topic of Urban Transportation. I presume that all of you have read the extremely provocative document which was distributed as a part of the background for this symposium. You will note that the paper poses five broad issues for discussion. In its introductory section on the first page, it also emphasizes that the symposium should be a consideration of action rather than a debate about the background philosophy. Given the advantages offered by the resource people here, both in government and from two major transit operations, what might we develop here, from your standpoint as businessmen, in the way of alternative courses of action? I emphasize the term "action" again because I think many of us are frustrated by the continual study and lack of action—the continual talk about urban transportation and the lack of progress in better service to the communities.

So, again let me caution you that we do not want to divert the discussion to any lengthy debate about the background issues, whether public or private, or the role of the federal government or state government, or the role of subsidy at any level of government. These are issues, I think, that may affect a particular course of action and that may influence your evaluation of possible alternatives. But let's not spend our time in debating what has become an established fact—a federal role in urban transportation—and another established fact—that there are both private and public operations at the local level, and that there are a variety of mixes of public and private interest and public and private funds in this whole complex service that we call urban transportation.

I think basically there are three elements to consider. One is political in the broad sense of the development of public policy for a community. Once policy in terms of goals can be defined you have a tool for the development and reinforcement of public opinion. Secondly, we have the problem of financing. How do we go about it? Thirdly, and hopefully third in priority for this afternoon's discussion, is the problem of technology. What kind of hardware is adapted to providing the services that we expect of our urban transportation?

I think the general approach has been one of major emphasis upon hardware—the technology—sublimating the political process with the hope that a particular scheme or a particular proposal will emerge to solve the so-called urban transportation problem. Perhaps we should look at it from the other end, in the order of the political, the financial, and the technological aspects of this question.

With these very general and somewhat vague remarks, perhaps we should turn to the document to which you were exposed and point out the five issues that have been suggested here as the basis for discussion this afternoon. The first issue posed is the relationship of transportation to the urban area as a whole, and this I think we could categorize as the planning issue. Secondly, there is the issue of public versus private ownership, which is affecting the development of improved service in several metropolitan areas. Here is a conceptual issue. A third issue is: how is the transportation system to be evaluated? This is an issue around the general subject of criteria. Just what can be utilized as a standard against which any particular plan or any particular arrangement can be critically evaluated? Fourth, what technology or blend of technology should be used? Obviously this is one, I fear, we will not answer in short order. And finally, the various questions arising from the issue of the federal role in urban transportation.

Unless someone has a major disagreement or a suggestion for a better approach, I would suggest that we take these up in order.

THE PLANNERS

The discussion on planning was quite abstract. Most of the attention was focused on historical trends in land use rather than on the relationship of urban transportation to some of the urgent, socially and politically oriented problems of the city.

For example, there was a good deal of concern about whether transit leads or follows the development of land. One businessman queried:

> I'd like to ask a question that's always puzzled me. If you put in a good system do you get people to follow it so that you don't have a lot of cross-hauling? If you follow the people, you've got to figure out where people now live and supply them transportation. This is the approach a lot of cities have used.
>
> The only city I can think of that has been active in this area in recent years is Toronto. I don't know if anybody knows what their experience has been and what success they've had in putting in a

new, viable system. Have the people tended to move around it—
up and down their lines—which solves the problem of all this
cross-hauling?

George DeMent, General Manager of the Chicago Transit
Authority, responded to the question about Toronto:

Let me answer your question about Toronto. I should tell you
that the new line in Lower Danforth, which has just been opened,
was laid out in 1942. I was working for an engineering consulting
firm. I was sent up to Toronto and organized the engineering
department that designed it. While I was still there we laid out
Lower Danforth, and we laid out Yonge Street down to Market.
So this is not a new concept. It was a concept a long time ago.
It was designed really to serve the communities where people were
at that time, and they haven't changed much.

Now, Toronto has had a very excellent experience of new
apartment buildings going in along the Yonge Street line. It's
created some new tax revenues for them. So I think it shows that
a good line will attract people.

Mr. Donald Hyde, General Manager of the Cleveland Transit
System, felt that, although transportation generally follows land
development, a good rapid transit line can have a significant effect
on population distribution:

I think, generally speaking, the transportation follows. You do
find in Toronto that Yonge Street is a main artery. They put a
rapid transit under Yonge Street. You'll find there was tremendous
development that then took place along the 4½ mile Yonge Street
route, a development which in other cities might well have been
in the suburbs or somewhere further out. Although Lower Danforth just opened in February, the development has already
started. So the development has been following.

I think you've got a perfect example in the Cleveland area
where in fact the rapid transit was developed first. This was in the
Shaker Heights area. Shaker Heights was farm land owned by
the Van Sweringen brothers. They were pretty smart operators.
They wanted to create land value, so they built rapid transit out
to their farm land. Then they laid out the entire area—streets and
everything—to fit a pattern of rapid transit that would be on the
surface so that you wouldn't cross it every tenth of a mile or so.

There are roughly three crossings to a mile and there are three
stops to a mile as a result. When you get seven or eight miles from
downtown, the cars run at a higher speed. There the people
followed the transit, so it will work either way. Basically if you
give a high-quality transit—if you give a high-speed transit—I am
convinced that the people will follow it, regardless of whether you
build it on farm land or someplace else.

Another major concern of those concerned with planning was
the future of the core city. Donald Hyde stated the issue this way:

> George DeMent makes the observation that, by and large, rapid
> transit radiates from downtown, and this is true. This is the place
> for it. But that doesn't answer the question: what kind of down-
> towns do we want? Every now and then I hear differences of
> opinion about this.
>
> Chicago would never be what it is in terms of the CBD if it
> wasn't for the grade-separated transit. It couldn't be. Other cities
> say: we would like to have the ideal situation where you live
> right close to where you work. You can't have a CBD then, or
> at least not a very strong one.
> The CBD advocates have a theory that the whole metropolitan
> area depends upon the development of a strong central business
> district. "If we could have a strong central business district,"
> the argument runs, "then we could have fine suburbs, then we
> could have a cultural center, and so on. But we've got to have a
> strong central business district in order to draw the people that
> will develop the suburbs and the schools and the other things."
> This is one of the issues that has to be settled before we can
> talk meaningfully about the role of transit in the city.

Both points of view were taken during the discussion. One businessman had serious doubts regarding the future of the central
business district.

> I want to raise the question of whether the requirements of
> this country haven't changed basically from what they were 20 or
> 30 years ago, when one strong central core city accommodated a
> particular area. I think that with the population growth that we've
> had, and the automobiles, and the ease of access to different areas,
> a central core city ought to offer things such as a few retailing

outlets that provide a very widespread service, and a few special activities which require large facilities, such as legitimate theaters, or professional sports.

But in the towns with which I am familiar, like Detroit and Cleveland, there are a great many things downtown that don't need to be downtown—things that would be much more available to the people if they were in five or six or seven or eight outlying areas like Northland or other big suburban shopping centers. I wonder if we shouldn't move from central core cities to more of these strip cities. Isn't that what we should attune ourselves to and not try to develop superurban transportation systems? Have a legitimate amount of service in the downtown core city and let the rest of it funnel into the natural channels of convenience where your population is and has to be.

Another businessman took much the same point of view:

Several people have raised the issue of land use. I think that's going to become increasingly important to us because technology is advancing so fast. I question the concept of our central core cities in some respects. We're going to have TV telephones very soon; we are going to have good communications. I don't, for example, understand why U.S. Steel needs to have its headquarters in downtown Pittsburgh. I know that in New York ten years ago General Electric considered moving off into the suburbs where the people live.

There was not, however, unanimous agreement on the demise of downtown. As one businessman put it:

I'd like to speak again about the downtown area. The question was raised as to why the headquarters of a large company has to be in a downtown area. I was involved in a situation somewhat indirectly, where this problem had to be faced. The experience of those people who have moved out into the country led the particular corporation that I was mixed up in to stay downtown for the reason that the services are downtown. If you go out in the country, you've got to take [the services] right with you and this company could not afford to do it. Downtown you've got banking, you've got shopping, you've got department stores and other stores, you've got restaurants, you've got all of the services right there. You have to build them if you go out. In Hartford, the

insurance company that went out to the suburbs had to bring the
services with it. It becomes a matter of economics—of not being
able to afford to leave. You can do all the planning in the world,
but you cannot ignore the dollars-and-cents part of it, and business is going to make up its mind on that basis.

Another counterexample was cited, this one in Houston:

Just a few weeks ago we had a vivid example of this problem
when Shell Oil Company decided where to build a 47-story building in Houston. It was offered a very good deal approximately a
mile and a half from the central business district—a beautiful
park. The company wouldn't take the option because their employees didn't want to work there. They wanted to work in the
heart of the central business district so that they could get a few
minutes off for shopping. It was that important to them.

After all the arguments and counterarguments were heard, it
seemed fairly clear that the land use issue would not be resolved in
the near future, and that it certainly would not be the issue which
would bring divergent interest groups within the city together to
take action. On the contrary, it was suggested during the discussion
that studies of land use and the interrelationship of land use and
transportation systems frequently serve as a substitute for, rather
than an impetus to, action.

The exception, of course, comes when inadequacies in the urban
transportation network, or the core city as a whole, reach crisis
proportions. Baltimore was cited as a city where this had taken
place.

MODERATOR: There are many studies, and each study seems to
    lead to another one, and a great many needed improvements never
    get off the ground. I think Baltimore is an example of a city
    where there is a determined interest now to resolve some of the
    recommendations of a variety of studies and try to get something
    under way. Do you have any comments on that?

BUSINESSMAN: Your statement is very true. Of all the cities that
    are represented around the table, I dare say that we are in the
    worst position of them all, partly because of the people involved
    and partly because of the nature of the community in which we
    live. There has been a history of deterioration downtown until

within, say, the past five years. I suspect that the only solution for Baltimore is eventual ownership of the transit company by a municipal interest. This, however, poses a very serious financial problem which certainly we're not going to be able to solve here this afternoon.

The fact remains that the transit problems of most cities are not yet of crisis proportions, and hence that most of the activity in urban transportation reaches a dead end at the study stage.

The Transit Operators

Given a lack of public interest in improving the transit system as a whole, the managers of transit companies or authorities have to fend for themselves as best they can. In effect, they are forced to look at subproblems over which they have some control. During the discussion, two of these subproblems received most of the attention: technology choices and finance.

On the technology side, George DeMent was concerned with the role of the automobile:

> One of our basic problems is the private automobile and the relationship of the private automobile to our urban civilization. It seems to me that our planning in the past has always been to try to park every automobile within a quarter of a mile radius of our downtown area. As long as we continue to do that, all our efforts will be self-defeating.
>
> In all aspects of transportation planning, whether it be railroads, buses, or highways, we always tend to plan in terms of today's conditions. Yet when our system—it may be a ten-year system—gets completed, the conditions are entirely unrelated to the objectives we had in mind in our planning. So I think that we have to introduce a lot more imagination into planning and direct it particularly toward developing some modus vivendi between the automobile and our urban civilization.
>
> The thing that I talk about when I make talks on transit in general is that, in my limited experience with rapid transit, people are going to drive part way. This you might just as well accept. It's a fact and it's going to stay that way.
>
> We extended a line for five miles out into the village of Skokie, which is the fastest growing, and now the largest, suburban com-

munity around Chicago. We put in 350 car spaces for parking, charging a quarter a day. This was on property we acquired when we bought some utilities. The day it was opened it was overloaded. We had to close the gates. We couldn't let them in after 7:30 in the morning. We've expanded that now to 520 car spaces. I was out there at 8 o'clock ten days ago. At 8 o'clock they were searching for a space.

I know Don [Hyde] is doing this on the extension out to the airport at Cleveland. He has two lots that have 1,250 car spaces in each of two stations. San Francisco has some lots with over 2,000 car spaces. This allows people to drive from their home to a facility. I think this has to be the trend and we've got to do it.

I'm examining now a lot where we've got spaces for 400 cars. It's loaded at 7 o'clock, and maybe we can double-deck it. This is a matter of financing. How do you do it? I can't do it out of the fare box as I know it now. This is what we have to resolve.

But we've got to intercept them out someplace so that we don't just mess up the inner core and so that we do keep the expressways for those people who have to use them. There are a lot of people who have to use the expressways.

Mr. DeMent went on to say that, far from being in conflict, the transit and highway interests in a city should complement one another, and that the key was not rail vs. rubber, but grade-separated rights of way:

Let me talk a little bit about Chicago. I was Commissioner of Public Works for nine years and in charge of building the city's portion of the expressway system. Way back at least 15 years ago the state highway engineer and I were in complete agreement, after getting many traffic studies, that the highways would not do the job. We were told that the day Northwest or Kennedy opened, it would be overloaded for about three miles. We felt that we had to do something to supplement the highways because the highways are needed.

I would say that, in my judgment and many people's judgment, there should be no contest between commuter railroads and Chicago's rapid-transit system. It has become less and less a contest in the last three years. We're supplementing one another. There should be no contest between rapid transit or mass transit and expressways. I'm extremely proud of whatever part I had in this expressway when I see, in the rush hour, practically one solid lane of trucks. They move in and around the city in excellent fashion. So we cannot forget the fact that we need expressways, not only for people, but for goods. And if we're going to make them available for those purposes, then we have got to get some decent rapid transit.

In Chicago we haul about 1,700,000 people a day on our mass transit system. Seventy-eight per cent of them are hauled in buses or surface vehicles of one kind or another. We have some 20 express buses with varying distances between stops.

We also have 200 miles of single track which would probably break down into something like 75 route miles of rapid transit. Twenty-two per cent of the people ride on that. I don't know the exact figures, but most of the people who ride rapid transit want to go to the central business area.

The people who want to come in to the central business district are very much the people that live in the city or in the immediate suburbs around the city. Rapid transit is pretty much a downtown facility. We haul 350,000 people downtown a day. This is about what we have as a peak concentration in the Loop. Eighty-seven per cent of the people that come into the Loop area come by grade-separated facilities—that is rapid transit or commuter railroad.

The other day someone said that we shouldn't always be talking about steel wheels and so forth. I agree with that. But there are a lot of cities in this country that need rapid transit today. And by rapid transit I mean grade-separated rights-of-way. Whether the concentration of people is enough to put in steel rails or whether you can handle it by buses on private rights-of-way— that is for the individual city to decide. But I think we need grade-separated, private rights-of-way to move people in and around the city.

As indicated above, a big factor in the technology choice is financing. The fact that there exist well-established mechanisms for financing highways, and that such mechanisms do not exist for rapid transit, certainly enters into the technology decision. John Kohl made this point quite clearly:

Is not one of the basic problems—and here is a matter that I think should be of vital interest to the business community—the manner in which such transportation facilities can be provided during the period when traffic is developing? Some means of financing must be found if transportation is going to play an active role in the implementation of plans. I think that we have in large measure solved this with the highway network. This we have financed, at least for the major arteries, from user charges. But we have nothing like this available in the field of public transportation. The fare box, as George [DeMent] said, is not adequate to underwrite the major capital needs for expansion. There is a period, during which traffic must develop, in which there are operating deficits. We have no provision for handling this period.

If we design the transportation system so that it follows the people, we establish a pattern dependent upon the private automobile. We do not develop adequate transit use to cover the costs of the operation, let alone the cost of the capital investment. Is there not a need for certain new concepts—a new recognition of the role, perhaps, of public support for these operations? Or should we stick to the traditional business evaluation: if the users won't pay for it, let it go by the board?

Financing may be a big impediment to taking action on any transit project. In the case of San Francisco, financing may now cripple a project in which the initial hurdle of drawing interest groups together has been overcome:

One of the biggest problems we're going to have is in this area of financing. I think the San Francisco transit people are being held up because of financing. They've dallied so long that their costs have gone up, and they're going to have to go to the voters for another allocation of funds. When this happens, it is going to stall everything. I urge you gentlemen: if you have a job, get on with it with today's technology and get it done. Then tomorrow we've got to face a new problem.

We're having a similar problem with urban redevelopment. One community in Pittsburgh was torn down completely. It lost all its tax revenues. Then the community almost went bankrupt and consequently no other community wanted to go through redevelopment. They said: "Look what happened over there." They're finding out now that you do this in small pieces. You do the part that you can afford and you get on with it. If you try to do these massive, area-wide things that take ten years of planning, you're going to overrun your cost estimate and you're not going to get the job done. You can't predict events ten years from now; at least I can't.

While important, the problems of technology choice and financing seem but a small part of the over-all problem of determining what functions the transportation system should serve, and how, given these functions, it should be evaluated. John Kohl raised the issue of evaluation, but no one responded to it. The businessmen present were as much a party to this oversight as the transit operators, and there was some indication that they too were having difficulty coming to grips with the transit problem as a whole.

THE BUSINESSMEN

The transit managers had no qualms about pointing out the businessman's lack of perspective and involvement. Donald Hyde led off:

> You know, I'm not so sure that business people know what they want. What brings on these suburban shopping centers? I'm not critical of the department stores for going out to the suburbs.
>
> Hudson's management, for example, says: "We run a fine store in the downtown area." Yet all of a sudden, because one store goes out [to the suburbs], and because of the competition between department stores, the others have got to go out. They just can't stand to see the other stores out there. This causes the satellite developments. They are not as strong as downtown.
>
> Then a certain department store in Cleveland screams at us because we don't run as much service up and down Euclid Avenue as we used to. This department store now has about five stores in the suburbs. Of course we don't run as much service downtown because there aren't as many people shopping there. That's one of the reasons.
>
> Without trying to find an answer, because I don't know one, I think that there is a need for business people to get together with the political forces and say: "What is good for the economic development of our community? How can we have a better community? How can we have a better tax base? How can we have better government? Do we want a stronger downtown, or do we want stronger suburbs?" This has a bearing upon transportation

and I don't think the business people as a whole concern themselves with it, except to complain because somebody else isn't doing what they particularly want.

And, on another occasion:

> We don't know what kind of a downtown we want. I discuss this with my friends in Cleveland. I ask them: "What do you want? Do you want more vehicles or do you want more people to increase your volume downtown?" Well, the answer is obvious. And then I shake my finger at them and say: "Now, what has been the position of your store this year, last year, or the last five years with respect to accommodating more people? Are you interested in making downtown more accessible to people or to vehicles?" Without exception the only thing the stores have been saying is: "Let's get more parking. Let's get more freeways. Let's do something that will get more vehicles on the streets."
>
> George [DeMent] knows that 87% of the people who travel to the Loop area of Chicago do so on grade-separated arteries. This is the only reason Chicago is the size that it is. In any other city, whether it's Dallas, or Detroit, or Cleveland, or Houston, you won't make progress until you can provide better accessibility for people instead of vehicles.

Turning to a different but related problem—that of the plant outside the core city—the following exchange took place:

BUSINESSMAN: Speaking as a businessman, I think the business community has got to be interested in urban transit. We employ 4,500 people in our Pittsburgh plant. Using the 1.6 factor,[1] I have got to park 3,000 cars a day. This costs a lot of money. If I can get mass transportation, or something, to bring them in or have them live closer so that they can walk to work, that's one thing.

From another standpoint, we have a payroll of about $32.5 million a year. If I can keep that payroll in that particular community, then I have a good voice in the politics. If I don't, those people will tax me to death because I don't have any vote whatsoever in the community.

MODERATOR: You raise an interesting point. You mentioned 3,000 parking spaces and how they are costing you a lot of money. Do you subsidize your employee parking?

---

[1] 1.6 passengers per automobile.

BUSINESSMAN: We are trying to provide what we can, yes.

MODERATOR: Do you make any contribution to their use of public transportation, or do they do that on their own?

BUSINESSMAN: No, they do that on their own. But I am wondering, shouldn't we? It might be cheaper for us to do this.

MODERATOR: Let me ask you: do you put up a shelter for them or something like that, to make it more convenient?

BUSINESSMAN: We don't have any good public transportation.

MR. HYDE: That brings up an interesting point. We have two plants, one of which wanted to know all about transportation when making the decision to locate in Cleveland. The other plant, in exactly the same business, said: "We don't want any part of transportation."

We went out to the second plant and said: "We want you to have good transportation or none. We want to go right to the door of your new plant. We want to have something really attractive." They had the finest roads for their trucks, but to heck with the employees. And, of course, they couldn't get employees. Then they came to us and said: "Oh, we must have transportation, and you couldn't provide the type of service we needed." These are the two extremes—two companies in the same business out on the same highway.

I've talked with some of those people. I've said: "What does it cost you to shovel the snow off your parking lot? What does it cost you for lighting, policing, and so forth? Is there anything that we can do together between us that will save you work?" We know better than to ask anybody to spend any of their money except to save money. So we take this approach, as business people to business people. "Can't we help you save money?"

Why, this is just a completely new thought to them. They couldn't spend any money for public transit for their employees. They say: "Why can't we let the guy walk for a half a block, or a block and a half or maybe for a quarter of a mile in the rain and the snow?" We asked them: "Wouldn't it be a lot nicer if we could just drop these men right off at your door, if you had a shelter there? How much money could you save? Did you ever take this total cost and divide it by the number of employees that use your parking lot and, figure out how much it costs per employee?" No! They hadn't figured it out.

Maybe we're too busy with our little problems, and as Dr. Schneider would say, we don't merchandise our own business. Maybe we should be spending more time with these people, showing them how they can save money. I think there are areas where something could be done.

Interestingly enough, most business representatives were willing to concede. As Lawrence Marcus, Vice President of Neiman-Marcus Co. in Dallas, put it:

I think businessmen don't really know what they want. There are many competitive businessmen who want different things. Houston is a good example. Josky's sold out a downtown store to Foley's and, by agreement, they couldn't reenter downtown for a certain period of time. They couldn't care less about what happens downtown. The merchants who made the decision that suburban stores are the way to satisfy people care a great deal about the arteries and the circumferential freeways and so forth.

Foley's for example, decided to add to its investment downtown, and they're very much concerned about what happens downtown. Retailers don't care, except that they want a concentration of customers in one place so they can afford to give a wide assortment of goods and services.

Neiman-Marcus offers an interesting example because we have two different situations in Dallas and Houston. Dallas is a city where over half of our business comes from out of town. As a result our downtown patronage is very good. Our suburban customers would like us to be in the suburbs, but we have enough business coming in downtown to make the downtown business a very healthy one. In Houston it's a completely different situation. There is practically no population south of Houston—being on the Gulf. So we're dependent purely on what's in the north and west quadrants. There, most of our customers would prefer not to come downtown, so we're in the process of moving and building our main store in the suburban area. We may even close our downtown store.

Another businessman was willing to go even further, and suggest that the fundamental difference was not between varying business interests but between the role of the businessman as a businessman and his role as a citizen:

The businessman has to decide which hat he is going to wear. Either he's going to be a businessman, or he is going to be a civic leader. As a civic leader, he will look to the core city for the cultural and all the other things we feel that you need in a core city. Once you make the decision that you are going at it from the civic man's viewpoint, then you apply your businessman's techniques to get the job done.

To me it resolves itself to this kind of a problem: most businessmen, whatever business they are in, don't want to get into the "wrangle" associated with civic activities, most of which are highly controversial. You can alienate a lot of customers if you take a strong stand on some civic issue.

The meager evidence of effective action by business all pointed in the direction of businessmen who were willing to become involved in the "wrangle." We have already cited the experience in Baltimore and San Francisco. George DeMent mentioned the work of David Kennedy in Chicago:

In Chicago we have formed a Citizens' Committee. David Kennedy, the president of the Continental National Bank, is the head of it. They are promoting a bond issue in Chicago, and part of the bond issue being promoted includes $28 million for extensions to the Kennedy Expressway. The highway engineers have provided the real estate for the right-of-way. This Citizens' Committee is doing the total job of selling this bond issue. It's a marvelous committee. David Kennedy is a quiet guy who goes about his business and works his head off. You wouldn't know that he is anybody or anything. But he is doing a great job for Chicago.

He also told of a realistic solution of the outlying plant problem:

In Chicago we have a large teletype plant that's outside of our normal routes. They wanted more transportation to their plant. We told them that our surveys indicated that we couldn't afford it. We have an arrangement with them so that we will run so many buses for them from the end of our normal line right into their plant wherever they say. We don't care where. Whatever we can't make up from the fares of those people, Teletype pays us. Some months they don't pay us anything because we come out all right. Other months they pay a small amount. This is an example of cooperation with big plants. I think they have a forward-looking management.

SUMMARY

While evidence of effective action by businessmen was meager indeed, perhaps more disturbing was their apparent lack of concern with some of the more far-reaching issues proposed for discussion. Going back to John Kohl's introductory remarks, the following issues were posed:

(1) What is the relationship of transportation to the urban area as a whole?
(2) Should we have public or private ownership?
(3) How is a transportation system to be evaluated?
(4) What blend of technology should be used, and how should it be financed?
(5) What is the significance of the increasing federal role?

Of these issues, the first was discussed strictly in terms of the historical relationship between land use and transit development. The second issue was touched upon only briefly. The third issue was never considered. The fourth issue was heavily debated. The fifth issue was ignored. In effect, the discussion group reversed John Kohl's original priorities: (1) politics, (2) financing, and (3) technology.

We are forced to conclude that things are not yet bad enough. Businessmen and transit operators seem to be viewing urban transportation as the problem rather than the city as the problem. They are thus led to focus on the problems of urban transportation—technology choices and financing problems—rather than looking at transportation as an integral part of a complex social and political system.

This is not a happy conclusion. But it is not unique to the transportation discussion, and it points up a theme which was further amplified in the discussion on social problems. The problems of the city will only be solved under the threat of crisis. Furthermore, businessmen will only become involved when that crisis directly threatens them. The threat, if it exists in urban transportation, has not yet been perceived.

Selected Bibliography

Danielson, Michael N. *Federal-Metropolitan Politics and the Commuter Crisis* (New York: Columbia University Press, 1965).

Meyer, John, J. Kain and M. Wohl. *The Urban Transportation Problem* (Cambridge: Harvard University Press, 1965).

Owen, Wilfred. *The Metropolitan Transportation Problem,* Rev. Ed. (Garden City: Doubleday Anchor Books, 1966).

Schneider, Lewis M. *Marketing Urban Mass Transit* (Boston: Harvard Business School, Division of Research, 1965).

Smerk, George M. *Urban Transportation: The Federal Role* (Bloomington: Indiana University Press, 1965).

CHAPTER VI

Education

Frustration was certainly the main theme of the discussion on education. It was the frustration expressed by businessmen in response to a government plea for help. The businessman did not feel he was in a position to help, and, furthermore, his limited experience told him that there was very little to be gained by trying. The blame for this unfortunate state of affairs shifted from the structure of government, to the school system, to the parents of children, to the Negro ministers, to the background and training of managers. But wherever the blame was placed, the answer came out the same: it's very difficult, as a businessman, to become effective in urban education.

In an attempt to get at some of the underlying causes of business frustration, this chapter will begin with the background paper distributed to the participants. The paper will be followed by some introductory remarks, first by Peter Muirhead—moderator and Director of the Bureau of Higher Education—and then by Representative John Brademas—one of the principal framers of the history-making Elementary and Secondary Education Act of 1965. These two sets of remarks constitute the plea. They will be followed by the business response: 90% frustration and 10% hope.

Background Paper

For every six children who begin public elementary school, two drop out before graduating from high school, two quit at the end of high school, one drops out of college, and one ends up with a college degree. These statistics standing alone raise a number of unsettling questions about the functions and accomplishments of education in America, particularly elementary and secondary education. The afternoon discussion on education will address itself to some of these questions, particularly to those which seem most relevant for business. As preparation for that discussion, this paper will first provide some background information. It will then identify the groups involved in elementary and secondary education, and will suggest some issues which arise out of the divergent interests of these groups. Finally, it will offer some possible courses of action for businessmen to take. These may be evaluated and augmented as the discussion proceeds.

INTRODUCTION

Elementary and secondary education is a big business. In 1964-1965, for example, about $20 billion was spent on 29,000 public school systems serving some 40 million students. Approximately 72% of these students were enrolled in 9.6% of the school systems. These are the large systems (over 3,000 students) which are designed primarily to serve the seven out of ten people who live in urban areas.

Focusing on the two-thirds of all students who go no further than high school, we must examine why half of them drop out of school before the 12th grade, and why none of them go on to college.

Looking first at dropouts, three major categories have been identified. Many dropouts are children who never meshed with the formal curriculum, and find themselves in the 8th and 9th grade instead of the 11th at the usual legal school-leaving age of 16. To them, school is a prison and escape is the objective. A second group consists of children who have special problems. They are in trouble with the law, emotionally disturbed, pregnant, forced to support their families, et cetera. The third, and perhaps most upsetting, group consists of those children who can do the work but who are not interested in it. They see little or no relationship between long division and the world in which they live. The more "disadvantaged" their environment, the more pronounced is their inability to relate. They do not see education as one of a series of natural steps leading to a meaningful career. So they leave. The frustrations of this group are probably shared by many of those who struggle through high school but are there only because their parents or relatives insist on their obtaining a high school diploma.

The ultimate result of the disenchantment of the young with school is a large number of United States citizens who are ill-matched to the job market. To see why this is so, we need only look at the structure of job opportunities and the shifting of that structure over time. The National Commission on Technology, Automation, and Economic Progress reports the following employment pattern:

	1947	1964	1975
Farm Workers	14.0%	6.3%	3.9%
Service Workers	10.4	13.2	14.1
White-Collar Workers	34.9	44.2	48.3
Blue-Collar Workers	40.7	36.3	33.7

The report continues: "There is little doubt that the occupational structure of the American labor force is changing and will continue to change. Perhaps the main reason for this is the rapid growth of those industries—education, finance, insurance, health, and business services—which employ predominantly white-collar and professional workers." The number of professional and technical jobs alone will jump from 8.6 million in 1964 to an estimated 13.2 million in 1975. If the Commission is correct when it claims that "in a slack labor market employers must have some means of selecting among numerous applicants, and it is not surprising that educational attainment is often used as a convenient yardstick, regardless of its direct relevance to the requirements of the job," the school dropout is in trouble. In fact, the person with only a high school degree may have a problem. The size of this group alone means that the problems of these individuals constitute a national challenge. And since business is the predominant employer of people in the country, business may be forced to take up that challenge whether it cares to or not.

THE INTEREST GROUPS INVOLVED

Everyone is interested in education, whether it is for themselves, their children, or their workers. To some degree many regard themselves as "experts" in education. For the purposes of this discussion, however, it will be helpful to focus on the few groups who are directly involved in determining what the nature of that education will be.

One group, of course, is made up of the parents of children. They pay taxes to support school systems, and they want to be certain that their children have the greatest possible educational opportunity. Particularly concerned are the parents of Negro children. It is not difficult to see why. The median years of school completed by the civilian labor force 18 years old and over by color and age in 1965 was:

Color	18-24	25-34	35-44	45-54	55-64	over 65
White	12.5	12.5	12.3	12.1	10.4	9.1
Nonwhite	11.9	11.6	10.2	8.6	7.5	6.3

If it is agreed that education is being used as an employment filter, and if we believe the Commission when it estimates that "if non-whites continue to hold the same proportion of jobs in each occupation as in 1964, the nonwhite unemployment rate in 1975 will be more then five times that for the labor force as a whole," the Negro parents' concern is understandable.

Naturally, the administrators and teachers in urban school systems are concerned. They have not been able to stimulate and motivate a large number of their students. There are many factors which might account for this shortcoming. First, the public school must depend primarily on tax revenues for support. Poorer communities must settle for poorer schools, or, in the words of Stanford's H. Thomas James: "The financial resources of a community and the quality of its population set boundaries beyond which even the most enthusiastic and efficient management cannot expect to move under existing arrangements." Second, there is little agreement among educational theorists as to how to make school curricula more challenging to a greater number of students. Third, even if there were agreement, and there were funds, there is some doubt about most school systems' ability to adapt to change. They are noted for conservatism. Many schools offer teachers tenure after two or three years of employment, building up a permanent staff with rigid views and little incentive or motivation to change them. When the school's product comes under attack, the school system tends to become defensive and withdrawn. This leads to the "snapshot-cocoon" approach. The school system takes a "snapshot" of the world, and then withdraws into its "cocoon" and bases its curriculum, methods, counseling, and facilities on that "snapshot." As one educator confided, "The problem is not education and the school system; it is education versus the school system."

Persons connected with institutions of higher learning are vitally concerned with elementary and secondary education. At present, they must take in students with widely varying backgrounds and then must put out some kind of uniform product. This is particularly true of land-grant schools. If they discriminate against the "disadvantaged," they are criticized. If their graduates do not perform well, they are criticized. Faced with this dilemma, they would like nothing better than an improvement in the quality of the high school graduate.

Government bodies have always been involved in education. Local government officials must raise funds, hire and support superintendents, and build facilities. Since a high percentage of most municipal budgets is spent on elementary and secondary education, the local government official's future may depend upon how well he performs these tasks.

The state role is less direct and has recently been the subject of much debate. In general, the states have provided some aid directly and have been responsible for allocating most federal funds. Using state departments of education to allocate federal funds was a deliberate move on the part of the federal government to bolster these departments. In the 1965 Elementary and Secondary Education Act, for example, the state departments take 1% of the Title I funds and 5% of the Title II funds which pass through their hands. In addition, there is a separate title—Title V—amounting to $25 million which is earmarked solely for support of state education departments.

This brings up the role of the federal government. On the surface, the federal government does not play a significant role. Of the roughly $20 billion spent annually on public elementary and secondary schools, federal expenditures account for only $1.9

billion or about 10%. These are deceiving figures, however. Approximately 90% of the total expenditures are routine in that they are for salaries, plant and equipment, operating expenses, et cetera. It is the allocation of the remaining 10% which causes most of the debate. This is the 10% which is spent on new equipment, on new teaching materials, or on experimental programs testing out new concepts. As the appropriations provided for in the 1965 Act turn into funds obligated to school systems, the federal share of the critical 10% may rise significantly. Thus the federal government is potentially in a strong position to influence the course of elementary and secondary education.

At present, the bulk of the 1965 Act funds (over $1 billion, funded under Title I) are directed at "educationally disadvantaged" schools. The allocation which any school district receives under Title I depends upon: (1) the average annual current expenditure per school child in the entire state, and (2) the number of school-age children in the district from families with annual incomes of less than $2,000 and the number in families receiving more than $2,000 annually from the program of Aid to Families with Dependent Children. This allocation reflects a federal objective, well stated recently by Commissioner of Education Harold Howe, "to make sure that the schools which serve our neediest citizens are at the very least equal to the schools that serve our most fortunate. In spite of local, state, and federal efforts, this is not now the case."

In response partly to the perceived inequities among school systems, other government agencies have undertaken specialized supplementary programs. The Office of Economic Opportunity, for example, has developed the Headstart Program to put disadvantaged preschool children on an equal footing with their more fortunate counterparts. Also, it has developed the Job Corps centers, which specialize in training high-school-aged young people —primarily dropouts from poor communities—to become employable citizens.

Finally, businessmen have taken some interest in elementary and secondary education. Their first interest has been in the wealthy suburban school systems where their children are being educated. Their second concern has been with the poorer school systems which fill their needs for unskilled and semiskilled, blue-collar workers, and has been directed primarily at the vocational programs of these schools. In assessing business participation, one must be careful not to confuse committee membership with action. In one city, for example, there is a business advisory board which makes recommendations on vocational education to the local school system. On the surface, this would appear to represent business interest. In fact, the full committee has not met for over a year and it is alleged that the committee was formed primarily to satisfy a clause in the 1963 Vocational Education Act requiring such a committee.

There is one group of businessmen who are vitally interested—those who sell products or services to the school systems. They are involved in developing teaching materials and equipment, and are thus experimenting with curricula in general. Potentially, they constitute a strong, innovative force.

On the whole, however, businessmen cannot be said to have shown much concern for urban education and as a result the businessman is not well attuned to some of the critical issues which arise in the elementary and secondary education field. Some of these issues may affect him directly in the not-too-distant future, and he must consider them carefully prior to formulating any plan of action.

THE ISSUES

The current widespread interest in the "educationally disadvantaged" and what should be done for them raises a number of issues. Clearly, this interest is correlated with the civil rights movement. The educationally disadvantaged school system usually turns out to be a segregated, Negro school system. It is currently popular for educators to be concerned with this problem. Sidney Marland, the respected superintendent of the Pittsburgh school system, has claimed that his Number 1 objective is racial balance in the Pittsburgh school system. Commissioner Howe asserts that "elimination of segregation from the schools is the most critical issue facing American education." Are integrated schools a worthwhile objective? Should equality of educational opportunity necessarily be equated with racial balance? Does education begin after 4:00 p.m. as some Negro leaders claim, and will forced integration of school systems lead to a mixing of children after 4:00 p.m.? If we take integrated schools as an objective, is it possible to integrate a school by building new facilities on the boundaries between Negro and white communities or will such new schools merely change the residential patterns, leading once again to segregation? If we choose to force integration by busing children from segregated neighborhoods to integrated schools, will we be doing the disadvantaged child a favor by placing him in a foreign, possibly hostile environment? Also, how many suburban parents will be willing to pay suburban taxes and have their children bused the other way? Finally, and perhaps most important, for our purposes, is it possible that all the commotion about equality of education serves to cloud some more fundamental issues about the quality of that education? As one Boston educator put it: "Should we be concerned with making Roxbury [largely Negro] schools as good as the best schools in Boston, when everyone knows that these 'best' schools are doing an inadequate job?"

If we address ourselves to the quality problem, we are forced to ask immediately: what should be the function or objective of a school system? There is a variety of opinion on this issue. One group consists of academically oriented individuals who contend that the school should serve primarily to develop the child's mind so that he will be better able to cope with the world when he graduates. Another group, as represented by Eli Ginzberg of Columbia, feels that "the school is the transitional environment between the sheltered family and the competitive work place. With this role, the school has always served as a preparatory training ground for employment."

These groups are not diametrically opposed to one another. Rather they disagree as to where the emphasis should be placed in the curriculum, particularly with regard to vocational education. Those who argue that the school should train minds, are likely to take the position of the Commission on Technology, Automation and Economic Progress: "For most secondary school pupils, vocational training should be deferred until after high school. The school should emphasize broad general education in language, literature, mathematics and science, history and social studies, and the arts. These subjects are an essential foundation not only for personal development and citizenship, but also for most vocations."

Those who believe that the school should serve as a medium for transition are likely to point to the dropouts and to the dissatisfied, and to note that these students do not see the relevance of the subjects mentioned above, particularly if they come from disadvantaged neighborhoods. The position is taken that unless the school can be designed in such a way that most students perceive it as stimulating, then the school is not serving its function. When asked whether more vocational education will serve this purpose, however, this group is usually forced to back off and to say that vocational education, as it is now practiced, is not the answer either.

This brings us to a basic issue: what is vocational education and what should it be? In most school systems, vocational education is designed to prepare the majority of students (usually 50%-70%) as craftsmen or technicians. Does this type of training link the home to the competitive work environment, particularly when a good deal of the training is done on obsolete equipment within the school? Or does it merely serve to separate the "bright" students from the "dumb" students, and then give the "dumb" ones something to do until they reach the dropout age? If you feel that most existing vocational programs are not fulfilling a need, what alternatives do you suggest? How do you propose to give a child the incentive and the perspective which will motivate him to obtain the background he needs for the challenging jobs of tomorrow, and what is that background? A few possibilities will be mentioned shortly.

Intimately related to the type of education is the amount. All too often in education, quality is confused with quantity—the more the better. The advocates of free compulsory public education through the 14th grade appear to favor quantity as an objective. Under the quantity approach, everyone who gets less than the minimum standard amount is a dropout, and becomes, for the most part, an unwanted citizen. To a great degree, business, by using the high school diploma as a filtering device in a slack labor market, is responsible for this attitude. Is there something magical about 12 years of education? Is there any reason why all American citizens should have that much? Certainly not all jobs require it. In fact, it has been suggested that one of the greatest causes of dissatisfaction among any work force is overeducation—there are not enough jobs in which the challenge matches the education and training of the worker. Has there been a good match between the number of workers with X years of schooling and the number of jobs requiring X years of schooling, and, if not, why not, and what do you propose be done about it?

The federal government's involvement in all of these issues, particularly through the Vocational Act of 1963 and the Elementary and Secondary Education Act of 1965, raises some fundamental issues. The minority group for the House Education and Labor Committee has the following to say about the 1965 Act: "The true purpose of this bill is to authorize general aid without regard to need, and the clear intent is to radically change our historic structure of education by a dramatic shift of power to the federal level." While you may feel that this is an overstatement, it certainly cannot be denied that the federal government is deeply involved in structuring education. Will this federal involvement lead to a local school system which will meet the needs of the local community, and, if so, how are federal administrators to become aware of the separate needs of the 29,000 operating public school systems? If, instead of detailed involvement, the government relies on uniform minimum standards regarding the amount and type of education for all communities, who is to be given the authority to set these standards, and will the effect of the standards be to lower the quality of the outstanding schools at the expense of getting the job done?

These are but a few of the most critical issues which must be raised and resolved before formulating any plan of action.

OBJECTIVES AND COURSES OF ACTION

The urban businessman has a big stake in education. At one level, he needs a properly trained work force. On another level, he lives in an urban area which he shares with the "disadvantaged." A significant factor contributing to the unrest of these disadvantaged is their perceived lack of a "decent education." Finally, education is a big and rapidly expanding business. The businessman's objectives will be tempered by whichever of these aspects of education affects him most directly.

If the businessman's objective is to improve the caliber of the work force at all levels, then his primary interest will be to work with the local school board and the school system administrators to develop an adequate curriculum. A few cities have experimented, most successfully, with business participation in a number of ways. One alternative is to have students work part-time and study part-time. Chicago and New York, for example, have developed outstanding programs along this line. In effect, vocational education is revised so that the school offers the basic education and the company concurrently offers the motivation, the perspective, and sometimes the money to keep the student interested in his school work. Labor unions, by the way, have actively encouraged this type of program.

Another approach is to have company employees teach in the schools. This has been particularly valuable in the technical fields. Westinghouse, for example, regularly sends scientists and engineers to Pittsburgh high schools to teach basic courses in physics and vocational courses in electronics.

Rather than participating directly in school activities, many firms have assisted by providing funds so that the school can hire a consultant to write an acceptable proposal for a Title I project under the 1965 Act. This was done for the Springfield, Massachusetts, school system by a businessman in that city. Others have established scholarship funds so that bright but poor students are offered a way to break out of their environment. Finally, a few have taken a hard look at the educational requirements of the jobs which they offer, realizing that a man with only ten years of education may perform better on a job requiring only ten years of education than a man with twelve, or fourteen, or sixteen years in a school system.

If the businessman's objective is to work on the problem of providing the disadvantaged with a good education, his chances of being able to work directly with local schools are less. Equality in the school system is primarily a political issue, involving city finances and political pressures of a high order. Perhaps the most effective approach is to join with others in support of a candidate for the school board.

If one is considering business opportunities in the education field, careful attention must be given to the customer. Many businessmen have found that the conservatism of most local school systems leads them to avoid the use of any educational product which is not a thoroughly demonstrated success. In effect, this has meant that new products must be developed and tested in places other than public school systems, and that the federal money pouring into public schools is not generally available for such development and testing work. A number of companies have turned to the Department of Defense for support. According to some reports, DOD is willing to experiment with new equipment at its training facilities. Because its funding is centralized, DOD is also able to offer the necessary sums of money required for development work. Federal aid to schools, in contrast, is so widely dispersed that large lump sums are usually not available. The opportunities being offered by DOD will be described during a two-day conference, arranged by DOD's Office of Education, on June 14-15, 1966.

When a new educational product is developed and tested, there may still be a problem. Most school systems will not use it because it is new and other school systems are not using it. Not many principals want to face a mother whose child did not get into college because "Johnny had to use that new approach and didn't learn anything." The marketing challenge then becomes one of finding innovative schools and persuading them to use the product. It is a long road from the inception of a brilliant educational idea to its widespread application.

SUMMARY

It is not expected that in two hours you will be able to cover all of the issues raised in this brief paper. In all likelihood, as you bring your experience to bear on the problem, additional issues will be generated. The discussion is being structured, however, to extend beyond issues. The object of the conference is to develop clearly defined courses of action for you, as business leaders, to consider. You may not reach a consensus as to which course of action is best, but it is hoped that you will go away knowing the implications of each alternative for you, your firm, and your urban area.

Discussion

INTRODUCTORY REMARKS BY PETER MUIRHEAD

It seems to me, at this particular moment in time, that we couldn't introduce a topic that is more timely than the problem of education and, at this particular moment, the problems of the federal interest in education. It's as timely as this morning's copy of the *Wall Street Journal* or the *New York Times*. And well it should be because the topic that we are engaged in this afternoon is the fastest growing activity in the American economy.

I won't outrage you with statistics, but, in the course of the past ten years, the total educational enterprise in this nation has increased from about $21 billion to $43 billion. The projections are that in the next ten years it will reach the level of $60 billion. More than 46 million young people attend our elementary and secondary schools and our colleges. It involves 125,000 schools, 2,000 colleges, and 2 million teachers. All in all it's a business that touches directly one-fourth of the American population in one way or another. Fifty-five million young people and adults are engaged in the educational enterprise.

So it should come as no great surprise that the Harvard Business School and the administration in Washington thought it well to gather together here some of the leaders in American industry and engage their interest in the problems of education that face us today.

The federal interest in education in coming alive. It is coming alive a little belatedly, perhaps, but nevertheless there is strong and convincing evidence that it is coming alive, and for a great many reasons. Probably the most compelling reason is that at last there seems to be a sort of consensus in this nation: that if we are going to strengthen the muscle and fiber of the American education system it will take access to all the resources we have—state, local and federal. One of the reasons why it has not come alive sooner, I think, is because the Congress very wisely deliberated over some of the deep-seated problems that reside in federal aid to education. All of us are concerned lest an increased federal role in education would lead to federal control. The Congress very wisely waited until there had emerged a consensus in this nation that the federal resources could be used without damaging what all of us want to cherish—that is, state and local autonomy and the freedom of institutions of higher education.

I think the federal interest has come alive too because the Congress has found that, with the passage of the Civil Rights Act, we have removed another deep-seated, very sensitive problem that stood in the way of using the federal resources.

And so we have come now, I think, to center stage, with a consensus emerging in the nation that the problems of education are deep-seated enough to warrant the use of the federal resources, and that all of us must stay on guard lest the use of those resources lead to federal control.

I think we would like this afternoon to direct our attention to what is probably one of the most pressing problems in American education. That is: what can we do to improve the quality of education for young people in disadvantaged areas? What can we do, to be very specific, to improve the quality of education for young people in the slum areas of our cities. Granted there are many problems besetting education, and I think it's fair to say that the federal government is not going to resolve all of them. But the Congress again, in what I consider to be its infinite wisdom, decided: let's get hold of this thing and let's take a bite-sized chunk; let's take the most pressing problem, and that is: can we use the federal resources to make a significant attack upon the poverty and deprivation that now exists so rampantly and so shockingly in many of our urban schools?

With all the glorious things that go on in education in America there are a number of very dismal things that go on. We find, for example, that the dropout rate for young people in the slum schools runs to 60%, as compared to the average dropout rate of 33⅓% in our nonslum schools or in our suburban schools.

We find that in our elementary and secondary schools, where there are now 42 million children, 5 million of them come from families that are earning less than $2,000 a year. We find that there is a high correlation between the problems of poverty and the problems of the Negro. The unemployment rate for Negro teen-agers— dropouts from high school—is four times greater than the unemployment rate for white teen-agers. The achievement rate for young people in slum schools falls from two to three and one-half grades behind their contemporaries in nonslum schools. These, I suggest to you, are the dismal statistics which prompted the Congress to pass the Elementary and Secondary Education Act of 1965. This is why it directed its prime attention to dealing with the problems of the slum schools.

We have with us this afternoon one of the leaders in the Labor and Education Committee, Mr. John Brademas. He has been a staunch advocate of strengthening American education in all of its parts and has played a leading role in the passage of the Elementary and Secondary Education Act. I thought there might be some advantage in having him tell us a little about what the thinking of Congress was as they moved toward the passage of this legislation.

Remarks by Representative John Brademas

Let me say first of all, ladies and gentlemen, that as a practicing politician I am delighted to see so many distinguished business and industrial leaders come to Washington to discuss the several subjects on your agenda, but I am particularly glad to see that you have such a deep interest in education.

Peter Muirhead, good politician that he is, has been much too generous to some of us in the legislative branch. I think a primary reason for the explosion of federal support for education in this country in the last few years has been the first-class leadership in the executive branch of government as well as, I hope it's fair to say, in the legislative branch. Both Presidents Kennedy and Johnson clearly felt very deeply about education. Frank Keppel, who is leaving the government, I'm unhappy to say, is one of the reasons that we were able to do so much. I urge all of you to go out and buy a copy of his just-published book, *The Necessary Revolution in American Education.*

Some of the reasons that went into justifying this very large expenditure of federal money—over a billion dollars under Title I of the Elementary and Secondary Education Act — are the same reasons that I hope will compel you as business and industrial leaders to give greater attention to supporting education in your own communities and within your own areas of responsibility. I am now addressing myself primarily to the question of education at the elementary and secondary level for poor people. We have a lot of semantics that we use around here—"culturally disadvantaged," for example—but what we are really talking about, as I see it, is poor people. And in very large measure, that means Negro Americans. Improving the education of children from poor families is, then, one of the reasons that we passed the bill.

Another justification for the legislation touches on the question of trained manpower in a tight labor market. You know better than I that you've got to have people who can read and write, and hopefully something beyond that, if you're going to be able to get the job done in American business and industry. I have sermons preached to me every time I go home by business and industrial leaders in my own area to the effect that they simply cannot get adequately trained men and women. So increasing the supply of trained manpower is another reason for the education measures.

There's another rather negative but nonetheless significant reason that ought to strike those of you who live in Chicago. When you have a lot of poorly trained, poorly educated people, the cost of welfare to a community is very high. Those of you who live in Cook County will have better figures than I on what I am sure must be the astronomical, phenomenal cost of welfare.

I want to interject another point about the question of race relations. If you have poor schools—and I've already suggested that in large measure this is going to mean that schools are bad in areas predominantly populated by Negroes—you're likely to have some very serious racial turmoil in your communities. Here is a problem where I think business and industrial leaders can be of enormous influence, because you are usually identified with the local establishment in any community and if, therefore, you show some anticipatory leadership, if you look down the road a little bit, you'll have infinitely more influence than will people who are identified as being professionally concerned with race relations.

There is another reason for greater support of education which I think is perhaps even more significant to you as businessmen. Well-trained people mean better markets. They mean better consumers. I am sure you realize that the higher the level of education and training of people in a community, the more likely they are to spend more money. They'll be better customers.

You as businessmen, then, should not forget the more we support education and the better our institutions of education, the better the market there will be for American business.

I think there is another reason that was central in the thinking of those of us who worked on this legislation. It is a profoundly moral reason. There was a great sense of injustice, I think, on the part of members of the Committee on Education and Labor in the House and of the Senate Labor and Public Welfare Committee, and indeed on the part of most members of Congress who supported this legislation. We felt that it was somehow not right that children in this country should be deprived of an opportunity to live up to the best that is in them. It's common knowledge and banal to repeat it, but it is nonetheless true, that if you have poor schools, children won't have a fair chance in life. Indeed, if you look at some of the public statements, especially some of the extemporaneous statements, of President Johnson when he is speaking about education, you will sense something of that very deep moral passion that the President feels about education.

I didn't mean to make so long a speech, but only to suggest some of the reasons that those of us in Congress who have been, and continue to be, strong champions of education legislation had in our minds as we passed it.

THE RESPONSE OF BUSINESS

The businessmen present found a number of reasons why they were unable to respond effectively to the problems outlined by

Peter Muirhead and John Brademas. Perhaps the greatest blame was placed on the structure of the urban environment. The most eloquent proponent of this view was Mr. Robert Ryan, President of the Regional Industrial Development Corporation in Pittsburgh:

> I'd like to pick up where Congressman Brademas left off. It seems to me that Congressman Brademas is concerned, as I am, with poor people. He's also concerned with the way in which the business community can help what he calls the "local establishment."
>
> A major point I would like to make is that, except for Los Angeles, which is a world of its own, all of the urban metropolitan areas in this country look alike. They look alike in this way: there is a central city and there are suburbs around the central city. Within the central city we have a downtown core, except for Los Angeles, and around the downtown core we have what Ray Vernon of the Harvard Business School has correctly described as the grey zone. The grey zone exists between the downtown core and the suburbs, but the grey zone is in the central city. It's also a fact that this grey zone is where most of our problems are—within the structure of the central city. This is where the poor, the indigent, the families in trouble, the welfare cases, and the nonwhites live. So I think it's extremely important that we identify where the greater part of our problem lies, which is in the grey zone of the central city, and that we identify who these problem people are. For the most part these are the poor people, and these are the nonwhites. That's my first point.
>
> My second point is that the business community does not live in the central city. What I mean by that is that businessmen long, long ago have fled to the suburbs. So, the businessmen don't live in the central cities where the problems are. The businessmen live somewhere else. When you talk to the individual businessman about making his influence felt, he is most likely to interpret that as meaning that he should make his influence felt in the suburb where that local school committee exists, and where he can participate, and where he knows the school teachers, and where his kids go to school.
>
> But you see, this is not the problem. My reaction to the background paper was that, while it does a very good job of reciting the problem, the background paper presumes that somehow or other the businessman can be effective, as things now stand, in

the area where the problem is. My thesis is that the businessman cannot be effective in the area where the problem is.

The fact of the matter is that we have a structural problem here. The structural problem is that the organization of local government is such that we have isolated the central city from the effectiveness of the businessman. The businessman, as a matter of fact, can do very little about that because he does not live there. It's fine for people to suggest that business advisory committees be formed to assist in the problems of the central city with respect to education. I would argue that the businessman finds himself today pretty ineffective in that central city because he does not have the mandate to do anything. He does not have the official position as a member of the school board, either elected or appointed, of that central city to do a darn thing about it.

What has concerned me a great deal in working in this field is this: I find that the businessman as a businessman has no hesitancy whatsoever to restructure his own corporate organizational structure. If his existing corporate organizational structure is not working, he changes it. He moves blocks around, he changes blocks, he changes lines of communication, he reorganizes the structure in order for it to be more efficient and more effective. However, when you ask the businessman if he considers that a reorganization of governmental structure is necessary to deal with the problem that we're discussing today, the businessman in general is reluctant to face up to this fact.

I am going to close right here simply by pointing out that I have noticed an inconsistency on the part of the average businessman. He will not face up to the structural, organizational problem as it relates to education and the urban areas. This is in contrast to his typical attitude with respect to organization and structure within his own corporate framework.

Not everyone present was satisfied with Mr. Ryan's analysis. As one man put it:

I'd like to ask Mr. Ryan whether he thinks the major problem is the kind of governmental structure that we have, with the emphasis on local communities. In Montgomery County I was surprised to find, for example, that we have a county system rather than a suburban system in terms of schools. Perhaps a more important consideration is that when you move from the city to the suburb, your emotional commitment is to your own community rather than to the problems of education in the central city, and that this is as much a block as any other to active business participation in central city education.

Secondly, I would like to ask him whether the issue is quite as simple as he poses it. Lexington [Massachusetts] was always considered to be sort of a garden spot, but we have our disadvantages in Lexington as well. I wonder if we can block it out quite as simply as the central city, which is poverty-stricken and in great misery, as opposed to the suburban areas which are so well off. My hunch is that you've got very serious pockets of disadvantaged all over these metropolitan areas, that they aren't just restricted to the cities, and that the businessman is going to find in his own very comfortable and affluent suburb plenty of opportunity to do something about disadvantaged communities if he wishes to do so.

Mr. Ryan responded by putting his views in historical perspective and by outlining how the federal government is going to assume initiative if no one else does:

Let me say that most central cities wish that they had the disadvantaged people of Lexington, Massachusetts. It seems to me that the big issue in our day is spreading the disadvantaged of the central city to garden spots like Lexington. This is the big fight right now. We cannot spread the disadvantaged of the central cities to Lexington. If we could, this problem would be a lot simpler.

I would like to point out something which apparently has missed the target. Thirty or forty years ago, if you turned back the clock, it was the central cities that had the good schools, and you wouldn't send your worst enemy's child to a typical suburban school. Within the period of 30 or 40 years, that has completely changed. It has been in the suburban schools where there has been the effort to experiment—where there has been this spontaneous kind of interest in trying new things. What has happened is that the emotional commitment of the businessman has shifted from the central city to the suburb where he lives. I would agree that it's this emotional commitment that is as important as anything else.

Again, to turn back the clock, even in the city of New York, if you look at New York after the turn of the century, there were businessmen participating in the affairs of the city of New York, including the Board of Education. This was true of every central city in this country at the turn of the century. This is not so any more. Now what is happening, and this is really the point that I want to get across, is that because of this shift of emotional commitment and because the problems are now pretty much isolated in the central city, the federal government is being forced to make a direct thrust right into the grey zones. If you don't believe this look at all the programs of OEO. Look at the War on Poverty! This is a direct thrust from the federal government right into the place where the pockets of poverty are and where the disadvantaged are.

The business community can say, as it does repeatedly, that it likes to solve problems at the local level; that it likes the idea of home rule; that it likes the idea of keeping the federal government out except in sort of an indirect way. What is happening, I'm saying, is that with the problems of the central city, especially the problems of education, coming to a head as they are, the federal government has no choice at all but to do what it's doing. And what it's doing is cutting through the structure and reaching from the federal government right into the places where the problems are. And, to a large measure, the businessman is sitting by and taking no part in this process.

Mr. Ryan's position was not without support:

I'm not at all sure that money is the biggest problem, if I heard Mr. Ryan right. The federal government, and apparently the United States, has said: "Education is very important—very crucial. We're going to spend some money on this thing." Now we're caught with a whole lot of ways to go about spending money and exercising power which, in a way, aren't related to the problem.

If I heard you right, Mr. Ryan, the nature of the problem relates to the grey areas and the authorities that deal with the grey area. They get in the way of a businessman who is trying to be effective, which, in my own experience, is dead right. If, on the assumption that we all charged out of here wanting to do something, Mr. Ryan is saying: "The hell with it, friend. You're not even going to be effective. The government structure—the way this money is being spent, the way things are done—is in the way."

Another group of businessmen felt that solving the structural problems would just bring the businessman face to face with a second insurmountable obstacle—the school system, with all its unwillingness to experiment and innovate.

A participant from Philadelphia put it:

The background paper touches on one point which I think is extremely important—namely, the structured nature of public education in most of our communities today and the reluctance to modify this structure and to undertake new ideas, new approaches, and so forth. I'm sure all of you, like myself, have seen this reflected many times over.

It was brought home to me again last night. I was talking to a young woman in Philadelphia who has been teaching for a couple of years. She went into teaching knowing fully what the salary scales were and what the problems were, but there was one problem she hadn't fully anticipated, and now she is leaving to become an airline stewardess.

This is the problem of frustration. She comes to teaching with a very fine educational background. She has all the latest equipment to be an effective teacher. On the other hand, she is finding that her attempts to get a new idea adopted by the public school system are very frustrating.

I happened to be closely allied with the school system for a while, and this school system made a study of the adoption of new teaching techniques. They were embarrassed for themselves in finding that they averaged seven years to adopt a new idea after it had been pretty well approved and espoused by the teaching colleges. But they were somewhat reconciled by the fact that the average around the United States at that time was something like twenty-six years.

I see, particularly in these disadvantaged areas, the need for a philosophy of trying to adapt the early grades of school to the attitudes these children develop after five, six, or seven years of knocking around on the streets. If you try to drive them into a highly structured 1st-, 2nd-, and 3rd-grade education such as we've traditionally had, this is like trying to herd a bunch of young buffalo calves through a turnstile. It isn't going to work.

I think that here is where businessmen find themselves frustrated. A businessman changes, adapts, tries new things, and if they don't work, he throws them out and tries something else. I'm afraid that too often the public school systems have not been willing to do this. How can government and businessmen bring about a change here? I think this is really the sensitive part of how you get children oriented to school and interested in school.

Still another group intimated that having solved the structural problem and having conditioned school administrators and teachers to become innovative, there would still remain a hostile, taxpaying public which is impossible to cope with. Particularly difficult are the parents of children. As one man put it:

> I don't think that the problem lies always and totally with the school system itself. My experience has been with a community and a school system that was very lively at adopting new ideas. It was quite experimental and innovative. Yet there is a certain substantial body of public resistance which school superintendents and school committee members, as pseudo-politicians with constituencies, have to be concerned about.

> As we all know, the sudden and unpredictable upheaval of a community against a system which they think is getting too innovative can be pretty devastating in terms of a bond issue. People don't mind your experimenting too much with the company organization of Procter & Gamble, but when you start fooling around with new techniques in the education of their children, they get pretty sensitive.

As someone else mentioned, the public reaction is not limited to parents of children attending a particular school. Virtually every major interest group in the community views education as its concern, and not all groups agree. The remarks of one Detroit businessman reveal the scope of this concern:

> In the city of Detroit we recently had a vote on funding for a community college and additional funding for the support of the school district. This was strongly supported by the Board of Commerce and by every other business-oriented group. It was defeated.

> It was defeated, at least in part, because the Negro ministers in the central city on the Sunday before the vote, which was on a

Monday or a Tuesday, spoke strongly against it. They spoke strongly against it on the basis, which I think was in part erroneous, that these community colleges were going to be outside the central city. At least one of them was going to be in it. Be that as it may, the defeat of the community college vote also took with it the defeat of the additional funding for the schools.

This leaves you with a certain feeling of frustration. What do you do? The Board of Commerce, which is the most conservative organization that I know anything about, in Detroit at least, strongly supported this thing, and so did the businessmen throughout the community. And, as we all know, it would have been in a substantial part paid for by business in the central city. But it was defeated.

As most of these things go, it certainly didn't get the support it would have gotten had most people realized that it might have been defeated. But nevertheless, a significant number of people were on record. Witness the fact that the people who were elected to be trustees of the community colleges—presently a rather dry office because they did not get any funding—were business leaders. They were elected overwhelmingly, but no money! This leaves you with frustration. What do you do next?

In effect, businessmen such as the one speaking above felt they had been forced into the realm of city politics, for which they had neither the taste nor the aptitude. One businessman got directly at this aspect of the problem:

As a businessman who cares, I get what the kids call a "hang-up" in terms of the scale of the problem, which seems to be increasing at an increasing rate, and the organizational methods of dealing with it. I get in trouble. I can't be effective because of some silly law that says I've got to be a resident of the community to do something.

I find I'm used to leverage from my business training. It takes as much time to put on a $2.00 dinner as a $200 dinner or a $5,000 dinner, and I'd rather play where I get more leverage.

We can't get more leverage in education because we're just not equipped to deal in this arena of big city schools, which are tremendously complex. The politicians know how to deal with them and some of the educators know how to deal with them. But the businessman is completely ill-equipped. I would side with Mr.

Ryan. We're just not equipped to deal with this. That's why we go on a suburban school board. We can't play in the big leagues. These problems are a lot different from what they were 60 years ago. This is big, it's complicated, and it's a lot more "public" than we're used to in business.

SOME SUGGESTIONS

In the midst of all this despair and frustration was found some hope. A few of the participants saw ways in which businessmen could contribute meaningfully as individuals and, in conjunction with other businessmen, at the community and state level.

Charles Tandy, president of the Tandy Corporation, described his personal crusade in Fort Worth, Texas:

> I'm head of a company that operates with about 2,500 employees. I feel very strongly about education.
>
> The public schools came to us early in the Distributive Education Program. As you know, the Distributive Education Program is for youngsters who probably are going to have to drop out of high school if they fail to get some sort of extra income. Their families have substandard incomes. In most cases, none of these children will go to college. We started out in the program some 20 years ago. We were one of the first companies in it. I'm pleased to say that they gave us a little recognition in the state of Texas last year because we've stayed with the program. I feel strongly about it.
>
> If you are familiar with distributive education, you will know that the school teachers show up at the job. They organize and they make sure that the students write themes and reports on their work. The students spend every morning in their schools. This type of program to me is one of the strongest ones, and why it hasn't been utilized in these other grey areas, I don't know.
>
> We're taking these youngsters in large numbers. There's no requirement that they'll stay with us. Most of the boys are, of course, off to the service after they finish high school. Some of them come back. Most of the girls get married and get pregnant and start having families. When they can't afford to support their families, they'll come back and work.
>
> Our company started with just a handful of people. We've grown to 2,500, and we'll do maybe $50 million of busi-

ness this year. I've had a burning desire to teach these people some of the things that I learned, and I don't know how I learned them. I'm trying to transmit to these people the profit incentive. Every employee we've got is on a bonus basis. We paid out a million and a half—almost two million—dollars of bonus money last year. These are high school graduates. We've discovered that the level of intelligence needed for most jobs doesn't require college graduates. So today this is not part of our requirements at all —to join us and to join our management training program. We've found that these young DE [Distributive Education] students come on and make fine workers. And we've added to their education.

At the community level, there were two positive suggestions. First, one businessman described PACE in Cleveland:

There's an organization in the city of Cleveland called PACE. I think that most of the people who belong to this organization live in Shaker Heights and outside of the city. I think most of them are businessmen. They have tried very hard to affect educational policies in the city of Cleveland as well as in surrounding areas. I think that they have given of their time and resources and skills more than could be asked.

But I think the point that he [Robert Ryan] is making is that there is a limit to what they can do in a city like Cleveland, where poor—and this mainly means Negroes—are moving in, the middle class is moving out, the tax rate is going up, and the tax resources are going down. Because of the type of student and the type of family moving into Cleveland, the needs are going up tremendously. These are the very practical types of considerations they face.

A second participant suggested that some of the techniques employed by private schools and charities to enlist business support might work effectively for the public school systems:

If his [Mr. Ryan's] solution to the problem is for me to move my family from the suburb to the city, he's quite correct in saying that I will not do it. On the other hand I don't see this as a necessary solution. I would offer two illustrations.

Number one, there is hardly a businessman that I know of who isn't involved in education, but he's involved in private education. Why? Because private education has had the organizational sense to mobilize whatever talent there is in the business community to work for it.

Secondly I point out that there's not a charitable operation that I know of that doesn't involve businessmen primarily. In our own case in Chicago, the Crusade of Mercy is not designed to support the suburbs; it is designed to support the inner city. Why has it been successful? Why is it going to raise $22 million this year? Why will it be more successful next year? Because it's had the organizational sense to mobilize whatever talent there is in business, wherever this talent may live, and put this effort to work on getting something done.

I understand the differences between private education and public education and the differences between public education and charitable causes. But I suspect you'd find an awful lot of people as anxious to pitch in and help in the area of public education as they are anxious to help in other activities that may not have anything to do with the immediate community in which they live.

At the state level, one man, with experience in the New York school system, commented on how the businessmen might benefit from strengthening and working with the state departments of education:

Title V of the ESEA-1965[1] is designated for one purpose only, and that is: "To strengthen state departments of education." It's fine to serve on a local school board, but it's awfully hard in the community where I live to know what is happening up in Tonawanda, New York, or out in Islip, Long Island. With a strong state education department (and I'm very happy we have one in Albany) we do know, and we pool all our experiences, and we get a lot of money.

Of the 50 states in the Union today, gentlemen, there are two states, one of which I know is represented here, which have no school board in its state capital—no state school board. The other 48 have them in varying degrees with various responsibilities and certainly with varying calibers and strength. Let's take our great neighbor Pennsylvania, which recently, under the aegis of busi-

---

[1] The 1965 Elementary and Secondary Education Act.

ness and Governor Scranton, just had a full-scale reorganization of its whole central state school board system. They said: "The dollars aren't going far enough. Here is Title V available to us under ESEA-1965. Let's be businesslike and let's get all the money we can so that the experiences of one little school board in one little corner of Pennsylvania can be known about in another corner."

The businessman can, at the state level, do a tremendous amount. In those states where you don't have any strong state-wide school board or something that can be strengthened, get out there and start working with your legislators, with your governor, with your administrative people. Because the money is there. Uncle Sam has that money in Title V and that is money well spent!

Philip Sprague, president of The Hays Corporation, presented probably the most optimistic and hopeful suggestions, and in so doing summarized many of the comments made during the discussion:

Where does the businessman come in? I think there are three things that I would like to throw on the table. Most businesses today would not be able to progress were it not for their research and development. R and D has become a sort of imperative, compelling part of business today. Without fear of contradiction, even from my good friend Peter Muirhead or any other educators here present, there's hardly any member of the economy today that's more conservative, that is more resistant to change in the status quo in their day-to-day living, than the average educator once he has tenure. That's well spelled out in the background paper.

The businessman can, at the local level, be the big taxpayer in the school district. Or he may be a perfectly innocent citizen who happens to have a lot of land and an expensive place on Long Island, or in Nassau, Suffolk, Westchester or Fairfield County, and pays a fair amount of taxes. Thus he has a power (money) position, if not an official (legal, board membership) position. Moreover, he has a degree of independence—an immunity from the pressures of elective office—and can, therefore, play a more daring and innovative role.

He can thus aid his school board in what business calls R and D and the educator calls experimentation. The most practical way of doing that, among others, is to see where he can make the educational dollar—whether it comes out of his own pocket directly, or indirectly through state taxes, or even more indirectly through the return from federal taxes—make the educational dollar go further.

Second, I think the businessman should get much more involved, particularly if he is beginning to live on the periphery of the core cities Mr. Ryan described. He can jump in instead of taking a defensive posture or no posture at all. Look at the alarmingly low number of people who participate in school board elections year-by-year. Instead of being always on the defensive, be on the offensive and become a leader in trying to see where in the whole metropolitan complex he can help solve the problems of education in the core city.

Finally, as Bob Weaver showed this morning, of all that is needed, money is the most important single factor because of the sheer scale of the problems. We as local taxpayers in Westchester or Winnetka or Michigan City can say it's getting pretty rough as far as the tax on real estate is concerned. Obviously the state budget in New York State is getting tighter and tighter. And not only in New York; it's getting true of other states, and still the funds available from state and local sources are inadequate in relationship to the size of the problem. Therefore federal money has got to come in, because the federal government (through that clever device of corporate and personal income taxes) is the only unit which has funds on the same order of magnitude as the problems. It's coming in from the federal government now. If we are to assure that the federal government remains a junior partner in education, as Frank Keppel said when he was commissioner, it behooves the business community to begin to find out how it can fit in and help the educators to the maximum extent possible to siphon this federal money into the most effective channels so that it will: (a) do the best job, and (b) keep Uncle Sam as a junior partner.

SUMMARY

The discussion on education ran head-on into a fundamental problem. To what extent should the businessman in a community have an interest in urban education, and, perhaps more significantly, to what extent should he feel an obligation to improve it. By and large, the businessmen present responded to the educator's plea for both an interest and an obligation by claiming that neither could be reasonably expected, given the way education is handled in the cities. To Peter Muirhead, this was not an acceptable answer:

> It seems to me that you are showing a good deal more humility than you should. The problems of education are complex and they are tough. But they're here and they are no more complex and nowhere near as tough as some of the problems that you've resolved yourselves in your own business. I say this without my educator's hat on. I say it just as you say it—as a citizen. You'd better find a way to help resolve some of these problems in education, because we need your help. We need the type of competence that you have. It doesn't reside in the schools. They need your help, and they need your ingenuity, and they need your brains. So don't hide behind what seems to me a sort of false reasoning that you can't do anything because of the system. It wouldn't stop you in your business.

Clearly the issue was not resolved in Washington on May 20—for education, or for any of the other topics. It may never be resolved across the board. There were enough illustrations of mutually beneficial bridges between business and education, however, to suggest that those businessmen and those educators who do get together can be effective in raising the educational standards of a city.

Selected Bibliography

Conant, J. B. *Slums and Suburbs* (New York: McGraw-Hill Book Co., 1961).

Keppel, F. *The Necessary Revolution in American Education* (New York: Harper & Row, 1966).

Kerber, August. *The Schools and the Urban Crisis: A Book of Readings* (New York: Holt, 1963).

Miller, H. L. and M. B. Smiley. *Education and the Metropolis* (New York: Hunter College Project TRUE, 1966).

Pressman, Harvey. "The Failure of the Public Schools," *Urban Education* (Vol. 2: No. 2, 1966).

Sexton, Patricia C. "City Schools: Though Other Issues Exist, the Basic Issues and Problems Arise from a Conflict of Interest Between Haves and Have Nots." *American Academy . . . Annals* (March 1964, pp. 95-106).

CHAPTER VII

Social Problems

The discussion on social problems left the impression that there is a great distance between the world of the businessman and the world where social problems are observed. The distance is so great, in most instances, that the businessman has not yet reached a state of frustration, as he has in housing and education. Rather, he seems confused and bewildered. He seems to be groping for some mechanism or approach by which he might begin to get in contact with a problem he does not understand.

Dr. Leonard Duhl, of the Department of Housing and Urban Development, moderated the discussion. He began by elaborating on the background paper and suggesting a few issues which he considered most important. His remarks will follow the background paper.

Not an insignificant part of the discussion was an early attempt to define the problem being discussed. After considerable effort, a working definition was derived, and the participants began searching for a mechanism or approach which would help them set objectives, organize effectively, and in the process, bring them into contact with the problem. It is not surprising that few examples of effective action were forthcoming. Some were mentioned, however, and they will be noted.

Background Paper

The explosive situation in Watts in the summer of 1965 brought into sharp focus the social unrest which has come to dominate segments of every major city in the United States. From the businessman's point of view, the most striking aspect of the Watts riot was the demonstration of resentment against the business community. The rioters attacked nonresident-owned business establishments, with the specific intention of destroying financial records. There are strong indications that the conditions which touched off Watts are to be found elsewhere: in Oakland, in Chicago, in New York, and, to some degree, in virtually every urban area. What causes these conditions? What are the merits of different strategies designed to cope with them? Should business become involved in attempts to solve social problems, and if so, how? These are a few of the questions to which the afternoon discussion group on social problems will address itself.

As preparation for that discussion, this paper will first present some background data. It will then identify the groups which are actively working on the solution of social problems, and will suggest some issues which arise out of the divergent interests of these groups. Finally, it will offer some possible courses of action which might be evaluated and augmented as the discussion proceeds.

INTRODUCTION

"Social problems" is a phrase which tends to be used by one group to describe certain unpleasant aspects of another group. The poor, unemployed, tubercular Negro on parole does not perceive himself as a social problem. He perceives himself as a human being in trouble, and more likely than not, he perceives certain "social problems" within the "Establishment" as the cause of his trouble.

When we talk of social problems, we will be talking as members of the Establishment looking the other way. As such, we observe that every urban area contains districts which we consider blighted. These areas are unpleasant to look at and are sometimes dangerous to walk or drive through. Frequently, these areas are in the immediate vicinity of the central business district.

To be more specific, observe the map of Pittsburgh (Exhibit 1). The cross-hatched areas have all the following characteristics (based on 1960 census data):

(1) Median family income less than $5,000.
(2) More than 60 new cases of tuberculosis reported per 100,000 people in 1958-1960.

EXHIBIT 1
Map of Pittsburgh Showing Blighted Areas

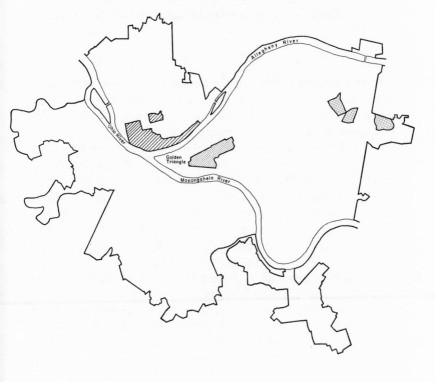

(3) More than 50% of the housing units deteriorated, dilapidated, or lacking plumbing facilities.

(4) More than 10% of the male civilian labor force unemployed.

(5) Median number of years of school completed (for persons 25 years old and over) less than 10.

(6) More than 20% of the population receiving public assistance.

(7) 45 or more per 1,000 in age group 10-17 charged with delinquency.

The dotted areas share the above characteristics and an additional one:

(8) More than 50% nonwhite.

It goes without saying that the boundaries of these areas could be extended considerably by ignoring or relaxing any one of the conditions. Note the proximity of two of the areas to the Golden Triangle—the symbol of the Pittsburgh Renaissance.

These areas have, or are, "social problems," depending upon your point of view. They are considered slums by the community as a whole. They drain tax dollars from the city and state budgets at a disproportionate rate. At the limit, their inner tensions explode out across their boundaries and threaten the continuity of city life.

The problems of these areas are not at all well understood. While there is a good deal of statistical information regarding the conditions of poverty, health, unemployment, crime, et cetera, there is little understanding of the processes by which these conditions interact to reinforce each other. Given the lack of understanding, it is difficult to design programs of action which will solve social problems. Despite the difficulties, a number of groups interested in social problems are attempting to take action.

THE GROUPS INVOLVED

First, there is a natural division according to economic class. At the bottom are the poor. As indicated above, they do not always perceive themselves as social problems. Many of them have never left their immediate neighborhoods. They are completely unable to relate to what they see in mass media, and many find nothing wrong with their present circumstances. As one Negro doctor in a slum area put it: "Our main problem is lack of awareness. If you want to see what I mean, try going down any alley and knock on any door. Ask the man who answers what's wrong with his back yard. He'll tell you: 'Man, there's nothing wrong with my back yard. They pick up the garbage every spring, right on time'."

In contrast with the poor is the middle class. By and large, their lot has been a gradually improving one. Most of them have moved far enough into the suburbs so that social problems no longer affect their daily lives, and they feel little compulsion to take action. The exception is the lower middle-class man who moved as far out as he could after World War II, only to watch his achievement being wiped out as his community became a "grey area." His land values have dropped, the quality of his children's schools has declined rapidly, and now he has nowhere to go. He finds that he is about to be reclassified as a social problem against his will.

Finally, there are the wealthy and the idealistic. To them, the city is a symbol of culture and the advancement of mankind. They are sentimentally attached to it. They do not want to see it "infested" with slum areas, and will go to great lengths to "move" (with a bulldozer if necessary) social problems away from that part of the city with which they identify.

Cutting across the economic class distinctions in any community are a number of local government agencies. Most obvious is the mayor's office. The mayor must remain sensitive to the political strength of the "disadvantaged." In most cities, they have been neither articulate nor organized. On the other hand, many racial groups are taking steps to correct that situation, and when the nonwhite population exceeds 50%, the mayor must be careful.

To assist him in controlling the outward manifestations of social disorder, the mayor has a police force. The policemen are usually in an uncomfortable position. If, on the one hand, they act as part of the "system," bending with the wind and handing out curbstone justice, they are accused of everything from corruption to unconstitutional behavior. If, on the other hand, they adhere rigidly to a professional code, they are viewed by the disadvantaged as symbols of the "haves" against the "have nots," and are unable to work constructively with local communities on social problems.

Attempting to fill the gap which the police might but frequently do not fill is a host of local groups. They include settlement houses, citizens' councils, local redevelopment authorities, mayors' commissions, individual poverty fighters, and branches of state welfare and unemployment agencies, to mention but a few. Many of them began long before the federal government became involved in fighting poverty. Each tends to have staked out a claim, and each is careful to see that no one jumps that claim.

Overlaying this multitude of local and state interest groups are the programs of the federal government. They divide roughly into three categories. First, there are the traditional programs of the Department of Health, Education, and Welfare. In F.Y. 1966, the combined activities of the Public Health Service and the Welfare Administration will amount to about $5 billion. In the words of Ellen Winston, Commissioner of Welfare, "The role of social welfare in the structure of our society traditionally has been one of patching up breakdowns and filling gaps."

Supplementing the HEW activities is the Office of Economic Opportunity. In contrast with HEW, the basic OEO strategy is to solve social problems by providing economic opportunities (jobs) and by providing the education and training necessary to take advantage of these opportunities. The War on Poverty, as the OEO's activities are sometimes described, is a relatively new operation and has F.Y. 1966 appropriations of approximately $1.5 billion.

Working in conjunction with these two major concentrations of effort are federal groups with special interests. The Labor Department, for example, supplements the OEO with its Manpower Development and Training Program. The President's newly formed Crime Commission has been assigned the awesome task of "inquiring into the causes of crime and the adequacy of the existing system of law enforcement, criminal justice, and corrections" and reporting its findings by January 1967.

Taken together, the federal, state, and local agencies present a bewildering array of sometimes cooperating, sometimes competing groups, all of whom are trying to solve social problems, and all of whom have a different definition of what a social problem is. It is no wonder that the businessmen in America have, in general, been somewhat cautious in their approach to the social aspects of city life. For the large, noncivic-minded firm, there has been little cause for direct action. Labor problems are handled through the union. Police protection is provided by the city. Delinquency is handled by the courts. The small merchant—the liquor store owner, for example—is not usually this far removed from social problems. He desperately needs protection from robbery and violence. In between these two extremes lie the majority of firms. They cannot afford to ignore the future of the city, but they are not dominated by the immediacy of social disorder. In this class are the department stores and the financial or service industries which rely heavily on large facilities in the central city. They want the central district to be an attractive place for workers to work and for shoppers to shop, and are primarily concerned with the blighted areas because they threaten to choke off the Central Business District. Also included in the majority is the businessman who has invested heavily in a suburb only to find that his investment is being undermined as the suburb becomes a grey area, or even a slum district.

Finally, there are the labor unions. In many industries, social unrest means labor unrest and the union leader gets caught in the middle. He is expected by management to maintain discipline, and is expected by the worker to act as the outlet for resentment against the Establishment.

THE ISSUES

In all the recent flurry of activity in the social area, there has been a tendency to lose sight of certain fundamental issues. They are the issues which must be considered in formulating any plan of action, and any action now being taken is implicitly resolving them, whether business likes the results or not.

First, we must honestly ask if the businessman should be interested in social problems as a businessman (as distinct from a citizen or a human being). Many businessmen have argued cogently that social problems are the responsibility of elected officials who represent the disadvantaged, and that direct action by business leaders would serve to undermine the basic process of government. These businessmen are particularly sensitive to those who would criticize them for using their power (as heads of large corporations) to influence social activity in such a way as to benefit the corporation.

If one takes the position that business, like every other group, must and should protect its interests, then it is possible to discern at least three good reasons for concern with and involvement in social problems. First, the problems are getting serious enough so that they pose a direct threat. Most obvious, of course, is the threat of crime and violence. More subtle and less visible is the gradual strangulation of the central city as it becomes ringed by grey areas and slums. If allowed to continue, such strangulation could wipe out the large investment by business in the central business district, and there is evidence that this is already taking place. In New York, for example, it can be argued that the high cost of maintaining social order coupled with a declining tax base due to urban decay has forced the city to turn to business as a source of revenue. The threat by the New York Stock Exchange to follow IBM out of the city reflects business' reaction to this turn of events.

Second, the solution of social problems offers a unique opportunity. Business is just beginning to realize the potential of the lower-class, nonwhite market. This is a market which has never been educated in consumer behavior. It has suffered the abuses of absentee ownership—grocery stores with no marked prices and 200% interest rates—for years. It may be the last consumer frontier in the United States in much the same way that an underdeveloped country represents such a frontier outside the United States.

The third reason for business concern is perhaps the most pervasive. Social problems lie at the heart of every other problem being discussed at this conference, with the possible exception of pollution. The housing problem is predominantly a social problem. Transportation is becoming one, as mobility assumes critical importance. The primary goal of educators today is racial balance in the school systems. If the businessman is at all interested in any aspect of city living, he can no longer afford to divorce the social aspects from the financial or brick-and-mortar aspects, and therein lies his predicament. Is he to try to separate them in his own mind, and act accordingly, or is he to plunge in with both feet and get up to his neck in the political tangle which is associated with any large-scale social activity? Can he act as a businessman during the day and as an aroused citizen after work? Or is it impossible to keep the two separated, and must he agree with Sol Linowitz of Xerox: "The fact is that the things corporations are doing are unmistakably of social benefit. And you can't separate me as a businessman from me as a human being."

If you become concerned with social problems, you must assess the merits of the various strategies which have been proposed to cope with them. By grossly oversimplifying the situation, we can distinguish three such strategies. First there is the "patch it up and keep it going because things are getting better" strategy. Most advocates of welfare and other forms of public assistance explicitly or implicitly take this point of view. Second, there is the strategy of providing opportunities and education so that the disadvantaged can break out of the environment which holds them captive. This is the approach of the Warriors on Poverty. Finally, there are those who would cope with social problems by containing them. The majority are in this last group. Their reaction to the high incidence of violent crimes in the slums and the spreading of these crimes into nonslum areas is more policemen and longer night sticks. Their reaction to the spreading grey areas is tighter zoning regulations, prohibitively expensive building codes, discriminatory housing practices, and the careful routing of public transportation facilities. It was not until Watts, and the threat of Watts' residents to go outside Watts this coming summer, that the containment strategy has been seriously questioned by urban populations as a whole.

It is clear that neither of the three strategies is self-sufficient. If you educate a young man and he breaks out of the slum, you must be prepared to patch up the aged and the sick whom he leaves behind. Similarly, you cannot expect crime to disappear with more welfare and more opportunities. To quote the President: "It has

been said that the fault lies in poor living conditions, limited education, and the denial of opportunity . . . . The long-run solution to
this view of crime is jobs, education, and hope. This is a goal to
which this country is now committed. But we should remember
that not all crime is committed by those who are impoverished or
those denied equal opportunity. In any event, we cannot postpone
our responsibility to act against crimes committed today."

Given that no single strategy is appropriate, how do you determine the proper blend for your community? How do you decide
whether a welfare payment or a job training program will do a
family the most good? How do you decide whether a Neighborhood
Youth Corps or two more policemen will have the greatest effect on
juvenile delinquency?

Since no one knows the answers to these questions with cer-
tainty, a third basic issue becomes important: to whom does the
businessman turn for advice? The obvious answer is the disadvantaged—the people who presumably have, or are, social problems.
The immediate response from everyone, except perhaps the disadvantaged, is that the disadvantaged do not know what they
need. It is not obvious from talking to the disadvantaged that this
is the case, and, in fact, at least one successful program has been
based on the responses of poor people to direct questions. The
businessman may be persuaded by an expert, however, that a more
sophisticated approach is called for.

If the expert works with a city group, he will recommend that
business turn to the city government. He will argue that the city
officials represent the people who have social problems and hence
are in the best position to serve them. He will neglect to mention,
however, that the city government is, after all, a political animal. It
must respond to local pressures. If the poor are inarticulate and
unorganized, and the middle class is large, vocal, and organized,
the city government must act accordingly. As one Negro resident
of Pittsburgh put it: "the blacker the neighborhood, the fewer the
city services and the greater the number of policemen."

Discouraged by local in-fighting, the businessman may turn to
the federal government. The natural place would be the Department of Health, Education, and Welfare, which is known for its

professional administration of welfare activities. He may be forced to agree with Commissioner Ellen Winston, however, that "our public assistance payments are so low that they merely perpetuate poverty." He may also be surprised to learn that in most states a mother and father must be separated before they can qualify for most forms of aid. Fathers have actually been prosecuted for returning to see their families.

The other major source of advice is the Office of Economic Opportunity. The OEO is not without its critics, however. It is most frequently called to task for not being in close contact with the poor and for administrative bumbling. Listed by the *New York Times* as a casualty in the war on poverty, Helen M. Harris, a respected social worker in New York's slum areas, gave the following reasons for her resignation: "It is always a clear day in Washington, and, by some God-given extrasensory perception, OEO staff can see what is needed in New York City, which individual group is best able to provide it, and which project should be processed first." On April 14 of this year, Sargent Shriver, OEO's director, "was booed, jostled and almost hooted down . . . while defending his program at a 'poor people's convention' " in Washington, to the delight of the local cynics.

It is probably fair to conclude that the sources of advice will never agree as to which strategy should dominate others, and, therefore, as to which organization should dominate others. It will be up to business to filter the competing claims and to decide on a proper blend.

When a blend has been chosen, and some action (to be discussed shortly) has been taken, how do you propose to measure whether or not you have accomplished anything? As a liquor-store owner, you may well watch the crime rate and use it as your criterion. As a civic-minded business leader with a broader interest in the city, what criterion do you suggest? Should it be some weighted combination of the eight factors listed earlier in this paper, and, if so, what should the weights be? If the eight factors are not descriptive of social problems, what factors are, and who will gather the data on those factors to keep track of their status?

These are but a few of the thorny issues which are intimately connected with social problems. The difficulty of resolving them has played a large part in business' hesitance to enter the social field. As the pressures mount for his participation, however, the businessman must consider them or they will be considered for him.

POSSIBLE COURSES OF ACTION

If, after you discuss the issues, you feel that business should definitely play a role in solving social problems and you have selected criteria against which to measure progress, you must then decide how to take action. One of the major objectives of the discussion will be to develop courses of action. As a starting point, it may be helpful to outline some of the steps which businessmen have taken.

Perhaps the most direct approach is to become elected to a public office. In this way, the businessman has a clear mandate to advocate and implement a course of action.

Less direct, but not necessarily less effective, is the work which business leaders can do with local agencies in an advisory capacity. As a member of the school board or the board of the local urban redevelopment authority, the business leader is in a better position to express his views without being criticized or abusing corporate power. This does not guarantee that he can avoid criticism as an educational expert or a housing expert, but that is another matter.

It is also possible for a businessman to work as an advisor to a federal agency, such as the OEO. In fact, the chances are good that a member of the OEO's Business Leadership Advisory Council will be attending the conference, and can comment on this approach. More action-oriented is business involvement in the Job Corps, where companies such as Litton Industries and Science Research Associates operate Job Corps training centers for high school dropouts and other "disadvantaged" children without jobs.

Many businesses are in a position to experiment with investments in slum or grey areas. The risks of absentee ownership in these areas are great, but so are the opportunities. A little consumer education can go a long way toward increasing sales and, from a social standpoint, increasing the effective income of the slum resident.

If a businessman does not feel that direct involvement with government agencies is in the best interest of his shareholders, but he wants to do something to save the central city, he might join with other business leaders to work on those socially related problems which might benefit from business know-how. The Greater Philadelphia Movement is a good example. Thirty business leaders have worked together in Philadelphia to turn a smoking dump surrounded by squatters' shacks into a $100 million food distribution center employing some 12,000 people and yielding $2 million a year to the city in tax revenue. This same group established an experimental diagnostic and relocation center for alcoholics on Skid Row, recommended significant administrative changes for the public school system which were adopted by the voters last May, and operated a leadership training program to prepare young executives for participation in public affairs.

Finally, the businessman may find existing approaches to social problems inadequate, and may wish to join with other businessmen to form a permanent organization which will develop and implement programs of its own. In Pittsburgh, for example, the Allegheny Conference has established ACTION-Housing, Inc., a private, nonprofit, civic organization. Originally, ACTION-Housing concentrated on middle-income housing. Lately it has responded to the social aspects of urban living with its Neighborhood Urban Extension Program. The use of an organization such as ACTION-Housing to serve as a buffer between the business world and the poor urban neighborhoods should be examined closely. For example, with what group within the poor neighborhood should it work? One Negro leader has commented: "The power structure within the Negro community is so complicated that it makes white politics look like child's play." By supporting a middle-income Negro group which is in direct conflict with poorer Negroes, business may be doing more harm than good.

SUMMARY

It is not expected that in two hours you will be able to cover all of the issues raised in this brief paper. In all likelihood, as you bring your experience to bear on the problem, additional issues will be generated. The discussion has been structured to extend beyond issues, however. The object of the conference is to develop clearly defined courses of action for you, as business leaders, to consider. You may not reach a consensus as to which course of action is best, but you should go away knowing the implications of each alternative for you, your firm, and your urban area.

Discussion

INTRODUCTORY REMARKS BY LEONARD DUHL

Every other topic of every other session at this conference bears relevance to the definition and delineation of any and all social problems; so housing, education, urban renewal, even transportation are part of social problems. I think the first question then is for us to look very carefully at what we mean by "the social problems of the city." What are the problems that we're talking about? Do they differ from the problems that we've been facing in the past? Then, very specifically, let's narrow it down to action questions. What action must be taken in the cities in order to cope with some of these issues today?

In every one of the speeches during the morning session, we heard allusions to the fact that we've got to find new ways of coping with problems. The old ways don't seem to be working. Some of us could talk an awful lot about problems of fragmentation in the city—about the fact that everybody's got his own little duchy and his own little empire, and that these duchies have not set up negotiations between each other so that they work together. This is only one of the social problems.

Another issue, in terms of action, is really: what is the responsibility of the business community in terms of dealing with the problems that arise? Are these issues that the business community should respond to? Should the businessman respond as a citizen? Should he respond to the opportunities for a big, new market of untapped size—those areas of the community that up to now have been undeveloped? Or is there a much larger civic responsibility that could be summarized by the words "consensual democracy" used in a speech this morning?

I wonder whether we can start by taking off from the paper on social problems, which I thought was quite good, and asking each one of us what we really think are the critical social problems facing urban communities. What are the issues facing you? How are they facing you? Why is each a crisis for your own particular community?

THE PROBLEM

The definition of the phrase "social problems" went through a rather interesting evolutionary cycle. It was first defined as a problem of indifference on all sides:

BUSINESSMAN: Turning to New York, I think one of the problems is . . . not quite indifference, but it approaches it on the part of many people. They don't identify themselves with the city. What strikes me as one of the things that keeps people from getting up and doing something is this feeling of being a little bit disassociated from it—even though when there is a specific problem and it rubs off in the form of a transit strike or whatever, you're very aware of it at that time. But most of the time it's not something that aggravates the people who can do something about it. The problem is indifference.

DR. DUHL: Can I just ask the question: What do you think indifference really is? Why should people be immobilized when, in a city like New York, you can be hit on the head with some kind of social problem almost every day, whether it's the transportation system, or whether you're walking in the street, or whether you happen to have help in your home, or whether you're in the schools, or what have you? What's the process which makes everybody so indifferent?

BUSINESSMAN: Well, part of it, for the average person I would think, would be an unsureness as to the mechanism by which he can get involved.

BUSINESSMAN: There's another facet of the problem. You're talking, I gather, about the upper income groups who just don't get concerned. But it seems to me even in the slum areas there's a lack of concern with the problem, because they've pretty much given up. At least the reports that I've seen indicate that, to get other than the militant few involved with improving their own neighborhood, it takes programs designed to reawaken the spirit.

I think there was some renewed interest in the slum areas last year because we discovered that the people were dead. They were just living death, so to speak, within the slum areas, and they didn't even do anything about their own plight.

When it became difficult to explain social problems in terms of indifference, attention shifted to the problem of differences in value structure between the poor and the nonpoor:

BUSINESSMAN: What basically is the problem? The problem clearly has a multiplicity of manifestations, but perhaps there is a single problem at its root. It has to do with the integration, if you will, of the lower income groups in our communities into the mainstream of the community itself—from an economic point of view and from a social point of view. Perhaps this is, in a sense, what we talk about when we say fragmentation. We say that there are excluded groups or areas within our communities which, one way or another, are not really in touch with the mainstream of the community's life or operations. How do you bring them back in touch?

It seems to me that the problem is one which is not solvable in terms of housing, or transportation, or education alone. My own estimate of the situation is that there is a cultural gap involved, and, quite frankly, I do not know how you come to grips with that kind of a problem. It's a question of fundamental differences in value structure between the groups. There are differences in conceptions of what is good and what is bad, what is desirable and what is undesirable. I think in many ways there are differences in the way in which the people who are in the mainstream of the community's affairs—those who are employed, those whose children are going to school, those who are not on welfare—look at the world. Their aspirations for the world, if you will, and their aspirations for themselves are different.

DR. DUHL: I heard you listing a whole set of symptoms. You were listing the symptoms of educational difficulties, health difficulties, difficulties of schooling and apathy, and everything else. And yet a listing of the symptoms and the implementation of symptomatic cures really doesn't solve the basic problems.

BUSINESSMAN: That is precisely what I am trying to say. I feel that the housing programs we talked about, the transportation programs we talked about, the employment opportunity programs we talked about, and things of this sort, are all symptomatic approaches to a fundamental problem which I see as a major, significant cultural differentiation between groups in the community. I for one do not see ways in which we can quickly bridge that cultural gap.

Finally, under the prodding of Assistant Secretary of HEW, Lisle Carter, the participants began to look at the middle class as partly responsible for the problem.

MR. CARTER: I hear two strains of discussion that leave me a little confused. There are two kinds of apathetic citizens, I gather. At least I thought I heard you talking about two. But they also tend to get blended into one. Maybe they ought to be blended together. But at least it should be clear what two groups of citizens we're talking about.

There is the apathy which typifies most city residents, regardless of their economic status. They feel relatively powerless and don't participate, for a variety of reasons, in any of the activities that might give them a feeling that they can do something about the condition of the city. Perhaps they don't feel these activities have any relevance to them. Since, however, this group does all of the usual middle-class things—they go to work, they have homes or apartments, and so forth—they are nonetheless considered to be a part of our main social structure.

Another group of citizens also happen to be poor, don't have regular jobs, and don't have decent housing. They, too, are apathetic. But since they don't have these other characteristics—regular employment, decent incomes, and housing—they are apparently considered to be somehow outside the pale of this acceptable main structure, even though the great mass of people who live in a community really take no more active and responsible role in the community—in the sense of affecting the direction of that community—than do these poor people.

DR. DUHL: These two are connected with each other.

MR. CARTER: I think they are. But I'm not sure that everybody here would agree that they are connected. While there has been general talk about apathy throughout the community, more specific concern about motivation and its lack has centered on poor, unemployed people. No one here has expressed concern about the lack of motivation of the average citizen who is apathetic and also solvent and self-sustaining.

BUSINESSMAN: I think perhaps I was a party to getting this whole thing started. Let me see if I can clarify it. Take the middle-class group to which you referred, and which I think, generally speaking, tends to be apathetic and unmotivated, or appears to be unmotivated. I have the feeling that many persons in this group feel that no real solution to the problems of the deprived group will be found until that group—the deprived group—develops a motivation different from its present motivation. I think that the middle-class group finds it difficult to conceive of ways in which they can take effective action toward changing or developing or enhancing the motivation.

MR. CARTER: I think what you're really doing is answering by defining the problem in a particular way. You are defining the social problem as if it is only a problem of people who are poor. You are not defining the problem as though it is a problem of the community, or as though it impinges on everybody in the community.

BUSINESSMAN: Perhaps I have not made myself clear. It certainly is a problem which impinges on the entire community. It is a problem which exists on my front doorstep. It exists in my neighbor's back yard at the very close personal level of burglary and things of that sort. This is a situation in which it is all too clear that the problem comes right back and roosts on our own doorstep. I did not mean to suggest that this is a problem that exists only in one section of town or that it does not impinge directly upon the entire community.

DR. DUHL: I wonder whether Lisle is suggesting, not only that these problems affect you—because crime affects you—but also that some of the very things we do because we're "in" people are problems. So what I am in part saying is that we ourselves, who presumably control the structure of government, the structure of access to universities and what have you, have certain problems about perceiving the rest of the world; and that the way we define our rules and regulations very often makes sure that these other people are problems.

Let me give you what I think is a beautiful example: public housing. If you look at public housing today, the rules and regulations that we, supposedly competent, people have set up for public housing guarantee that people in poverty are locked in.

The regulations that we in the United States have set up for the poor in terms of welfare and the way we perform welfare services have locked people into poverty. Our attitudes toward the poor as they come into the courts, in terms of the difference in the way the poor and the well-to-do are handled by the courts on such simple things as bail availability and a whole series of other aspects, separate out—"we" and "they."

BUSINESSMAN: Are you referring to the amounts of welfare payments when you say that?

DR. DUHL: No. When I talk about welfare, I'm not just talking about the amounts. I'm talking about the attitudes.

BUSINESSMAN: In raising that issue are you also challenging the mainstream? It was expressed in the paper somewhere that we have a mainstream and now we want to take this 20% and somehow bring them into the mainstream. What you are really challenging is the mainstream itself—as to whether the mainstream meets the need. Is that what you mean?

DR. DUHL: That's exactly the point. You see, I'm suggesting that the fact that we have poor today is a problem we have to solve because they're poor and because there are a lot of problems associated with them. I think the fact that they are poor also points up that there are inadequacies in our system for delivering services.

It was within this framework of mutual responsibility for the plight of the poor that the discussion continued.

THE SEARCH FOR A MECHANISM

It would be unrealistic, of course, to expect that improved definition alone would generate solutions, although, in this case, it helped considerably. There remained the big gap between those who needed help and those who might be able to provide it. The remainder of the discussion was focused on one aspect or another of how to bridge this gap. This phase of the discussion was started off by Dr. Duhl:

Getting back to a couple of comments that kept coming up over and over again this morning, one of the difficulties in the cities is that we do not have the mechanisms which permit the

citizens, the apathetic ones we talked about, and even the interested ones, to find expression for their concern—particularly
an expression whereby they can turn their concern into action.
This morning we heard several ways one could go about it. What
I am really pushing towards is: is one of the problems with which
we are concerned the lack of mechanisms in our urban communities
for defining problems, resolving problems, and involving people
from the communities in their resolution? What's really at stake
are the capabilities of our communities to finance this themselves
and to get a mechanism that works at their level.

Basic Concepts

It was clear to most of the participants that before searching
for a detailed mechanism, it was necessary to question some of the
basic concepts which have been implicit in many urban programs
to date. This led to a discussion of priorities and values. Two examples will suffice. The first is a discussion of the West End renewal
area in Boston:

DR. DUHL: Remember the West End of Boston?

DEAN BAKER: This is a very interesting area. I don't think that
the people who planned that forgot the people. They were just
terribly naive about what was good for people. They just decided
that it was bad to have all these people living in that area. It had
all kinds of bad social effects. It was a terrible place to live, and
it was better to get rid of it. The general idea in the press and
all around was that the project was socially, as well as financially,
very desirable for the city.

DR. DUHL: Actually what turned out was just the reverse. You
see, this happened to be the kind of slum which was really well
integrated. They [the planners] managed to destroy it. They
ended up with increased social welfare, court, and other costs.
They may have gotten beautiful houses down there and the water-
front may look a little better. They may have achieved some of
their goal, but at a tremendous price to the population.

DEAN BAKER: Was it because they gave no weight to the human
questions—the people questions—or because they took for
granted the common concepts of the times as to what was good
for people, and these hadn't obviously been proved? Was this
naiveté or was it: "we don't care"?

DR. DUHL: I'd say there were two things. First, in the hierarchy of values, the people value was much lower than the economic value. And, secondly, when they finally did move the people out of there, they didn't really give the people the kind of help that could have been given them so that they could continue businesses and find new ways of living. What happened was that everyone went into a tailspin.

DEAN BAKER: But before they made the decision, did they realize that probably, from a human happiness viewpoint, this was going to be bad rather than good.

DR. DUHL: At that time the answer was: "No." They were not considering that step. That had very low priority.

DEAN BAKER: I wasn't thinking of the priority. I was thinking: "Were their concepts wrong?" Did they think there was not conflict here, or were they aware of the conflict and did they come to the wrong conclusion?

DR. DUHL: They said this was a "slum," and a slum was therefore all bad.

MR. CARTER: I think that was the general approach.

DEAN BAKER: That was the general feeling. It was very naive. Here was a nice, warm community. Not much to look at, but certainly one where you could leave your kid with the person next door and know there was a happy warmth to the street—a human warmth to the street. And no one gave any weight to it at all.

The progress in Pittsburgh, described in the morning session by Mr. John Ryan, was also brought under scrutiny:

DEAN BAKER: The basic thing I always thought happened in Pittsburgh was that they got business leaders and political leaders and all other groups working together. What they worked on is not significant. I think once you get groups together and people are concerned equally, or fairly equally, about the issue, then it doesn't make too much difference what the issue is. You can get somewhere. What I keep coming back to is that here is a mechanism that was created. It could be used for any one of many problems.

BUSINESSMAN: Do you think they're so sophisticated in their approach that they have, in a sense, tucked away in the back of their minds pretty good ideas as to the balance of the importance of the various things they've worked on and, in effect, where they want to spend their money? Or has somebody said: "Housing is an obvious thing, so we'll do that. And smog is another thing." What has been the approach? Do you feel that they've really got a mechanism?

DR. DUHL: The answer is that I don't think they have a master plan in Pittsburgh and Allegheny County. What they do have is a mechanism and a process that they got going. Once this process started, it could face anything that came up. There were certain things that hit them first. The Golden Triangle was critical. ACTION-Housing became a very important mechanism for involving the big corporations and the labor unions and what have you. The hospital council was important because so many people were on the boards of the hospital. Then they began to move out.

Compare it to Detroit. You'll find Detroit has a different pattern, but it too is developing a similar type of mechanism. It is much more around a political base.

MR. CARTER: I don't think that we ought to oversell any one approach. I think Pittsburgh has probably done more significant things, for a large city, than any other large city in the country. But I don't know how much they have learned about ordering priorities and allocating resources.

DEAN BAKER: How can you do that? You've got to get a group of men—so-called leaders—together and let them fix their priorities. These priorities would depend on what their mothers' and fathers' attitudes were when they were kids, what they read as they grew up, and their responses to the pressures around them in life. There aren't any absolutes.

MR. CARTER: I think what you say is true when you're starting out. There isn't any point in having a big inventory when you first start out. Because there is so much to do, anything you do is worthwhile. Nonetheless, if we are working with limited resources, a time comes when we have to start making choices. They may not have to be made initially unless it's a very poor community.

DEAN BAKER: I suppose what you do is organize with these people who you think are good. You let them give the priorities and then, in a democracy, the political system determines whether the majority of the people agree these are the proper priorities. If you don't do that you really end up with the planners forcing down the throats of the voters what they think is best. I don't believe this is the way we've grown very strong in this country.

BUSINESSMAN: There is one question I wonder about. Did you say that Pittsburgh does have the mechanism that you're talking about, or the structure that you're talking about as being desirable?

DR. DUHL: Let's say that I agree with Lisle that I wouldn't put Pittsburgh up as the model because there is no great model in the United States. But if I compare it to a city like Chicago or New York, I'd say that Pittsburgh's got it!

To come back to something you were just saying. There is something very fascinating about being able to start with something physical that people can see—the fact that you can physically change the Golden Triangle, the fact that Ed Logue, when he was first in New Haven and then in Boston, could physically do things. But the critical thing is that once you start that way, you've then got to begin considering many of the social problems that we're concerned with. One of the great dangers of all this physical planning that's been done in the last 15 or 20 years has been that it's stayed as physical planning, and that was it! And we forgot the people.

BUSINESSMAN: Boston certainly has.

BUSINESSMAN: Perhaps we forgot the people before we ever got started. We've talked about creating a mechanism that can do various things. One of the things that comes right out of the bag is housing. I'm not sure that we don't make a great mistake by "doing" housing. I'm not sure that by taking an expedient approach to the problem we may not do great harm in undermining the motivation, the morale, and the value structure which, in the long run, I feel are the only real solutions to this whole bundle of problems. So that, in effect, in attempting to solve the problem we may be compounding it and prolonging it.

Possible Mechanisms

The discussion of Pittsburgh began to suggest one possible mechanism—a board of leaders whose success would depend upon some democratic process. The group analyzed this approach with remarkable thoroughness, taking off from the basic concept into all the difficulties of including the poor in the decision-making process:

MR. CARTER: What troubles me about the leaders-getting-together approach is that it makes assumptions about many different groups of people, and what their role is, and how they get into this process. I'm not even sure that the democratic process, as exercised through the ballot box, is a sufficient, or anywhere approaching a sufficient, guarantee that you're going to get the proper kind of feed-in from people who, if they don't participate in some fashion, are going to look at this as an "enemy" system.

DEAN BAKER: This gets into the question: if you work with a group of leaders—leaders of whom and from where? What you're arguing is that we should not think of leaders as just the top businessmen and top politicians, but a group that has the leaders of many, many groups. Is this right?

BUSINESSMAN: Has putting the poor on these Poverty Program jobs in the cities really added anything to the program, by and large? I don't know; I'm asking.

MR. CARTER: I think in some respects it has. But I don't think that's necessarily what I'm talking about, because I don't think the formal development of a board with people on it is the only way to get communication. I think there has been too much emphasis on the whole notion of having a board and putting people on it. That is not a solution in itself.

DEAN BAKER: What are the alternatives?

MR. CARTER: Well, I don't pretend that I know *the* alternative. But there are other ways of . . .

DEAN BAKER: That don't involve groups of people, whether they be leaders or not?

MR. CARTER: No. No. Don't misunderstand me. You have to begin with a group of people . . . .

DEAN BAKER: If you don't use a board—which was first described to me as something long and wooden—if you don't use a board, we are certainly talking about some group of human beings worrying about this. What kind of group can you reach for? I wouldn't for a minute say a board of business leaders is the only way. I wonder what the alternatives are that you're worried about.

MR. CARTER: I do not dissent from the view that a group of people who exert leadership in the community ought to come together around these problems as an initial step. What concerns me is the process by which they arrive at decisions about what happens in the community. In other words, I don't say that the first time a group of businessmen, or politicians, or both, or any other combination of people, want to talk about a problem, they've got to run out and get some poor people and pull them into the meeting and say: "Now, this is the kind of thing we want to talk about, and what do you think about this?" But, we have to find some way to afford people in the low-income group some mechanism by which they can understand what you want to do and are trying to do, and by which they can get some of their own feelings about their neighborhood and their community into the process.

DEAN BAKER: I'm still puzzled as to how you can do this if you don't do it by working with a leader or representative from that group of poor. It seems to me, off the top of my head, that one would think: "You ought to have a leader from that group of people." You end up with many leaders.

MR. CARTER: I just don't think even that's a sufficient solution.

DEAN BAKER: I gather not, and I just stop there in my thinking. How do those people, whose views you so badly need to have, get represented?

DR. DUHL: One mechanism is to put them all on one board. Presumably on that board these things get thrashed out. Another mechanism might be to set up a system where a continued confrontation process takes place between many groups in the community. If there is anything that I would say has happened to the cities by asking for "maximum feasible participation," it was not that the poor got on the board, but that they are raising enough of their voice so that the power groups have to respond by improving programs in a whole series of areas.

DEAN BAKER: Now you are getting a little more complicated. It seems to me that what you've said is that, rather than having a representative of say 20 different groups in the city sit together and struggle with things, it often works better to get a kind of confrontation between a group with a terriffic interest, and—what puzzles me—a confrontation with whom, and where, and in what form. With whom does this confrontation take place?

DR. DUHL: In Washington we had a beautiful example with the D.C. Crime Commission. It had two sets of meetings. The first set of meetings was a public hearing which they held in the departmental auditorium. They asked the citizens of the community to please come down and talk about crime. The departmental auditorium is a gigantic place and a few people came. Most of them were the good citizens of the community who are public spirited.

Then they said they would go out into the community. They brought the Crime Commission out to each one of the neighborhood centers and they asked the poor to really tell them: what's the problem of crime in your neighborhood? These meetings were like day and night. And the confrontation that took place in the second phase was a confrontation about the real problems. They found that the Negro population living in the poor section was just as concerned about crime as the people in the fancy part of the Northwest section who thought that all of crime was due to the Negroes over in the Northeast section. It's this kind of confrontation for which we really don't provide enough mechanisms in the cities.

DEAN BAKER: But any good leadership board could do this. This is a technique than can be used by a group of consultants, or by a board, a commission, or a group of leaders, or whatever you call it. Obviously it is a very much better one than simply depending on one leader from a group to say what that group cares about.

DR. DUHL: Let's look at the major social problems of our community. Let's look at urban renewal, public housing, highways, and schools, and health. What kinds of hearings are held on any one of these issues? Not one of them has a hearing that you can get the public to. I'm talking about the public that we are talking about now. It's written into the rules and regulations that there is supposed to be some kind of public hearing. But if you look at the highway hearings, it's never occurred.

DEAN BAKER: Who would oppose this kind of approach?

DR. DUHL: I once got up at a meeting and proposed this. It was a meeting of planners and highway officials. A gentleman got up and said: "Doctor, that's not the way to build a highway, because it takes too damn long. The only way to build a highway is to bulldoze right through." And that's the answer that you always get. This process is just too slow.

Even the perfectly run board, with a great deal of participation by the poor, would not be without its difficulties. As a group of people, it is a source of power, and power is the stuff of which politics is made. This difficulty was anticipated by Dean Baker:

I should think that, more difficult than getting this kind of thing started by people who care, is dealing with the problem as it begins to get in the way of the power structures that exist—such as the political system that has been responsible for running the city.

An actual example of the power problem was related by a Houston businessman:

BUSINESSMAN: I spent a lot of time talking to a lady down in Houston who runs an operation under a grant from the OEO. I have no way of appraising what she's told me. But the first thing they did when they got their grant was to go down into an area—largely a Negro and Mexican community—and try to identify the "leaders" in the area. They got a bunch of people together, and nothing happened. There was no enthusiasm, no response.

But out of this group of leaders there was a fellow whose name was Sam Price. I don't know if any of you know him. But Sam Price, according to this lady, has a great native ability to go through his community and pick out those people who really are influential, even though they're not the apparent leaders of the group. They spent a year just trying to identify these people and to get together a nucleus of individuals who could meet and talk and then have some response from the community. She says they are now getting it.

But the thing that troubles me personally is that the group is apparently now being pushed aside. At least, they feel that they are. I'm getting both sides. There's another group coming over from the mayor's office. What we've got is a great big run-in between the two. I'm trying to decide with which, if any, I'm going to join forces.

DEAN BAKER: It's sort of inevitable, isn't it? The original group becomes a real challenge.

MR. CARTER: Let's look at Mayor Cavanagh. He's been an exception in many respects. He's ahead of the game, so to speak. If a mayor sits back and somebody else does it all, all of a sudden the mayor sees a cohesion developing, and he becomes concerned. And this is not unnatural.

DEAN BAKER: From this, can we decide as a broad generalization, that you can't get far unless you start out working with the political group as well as other groups? This was one of the great strengths in Pittsburgh, wasn't it?

Another suggestion was to get a fresh attitude toward the social problems of the city by bringing in a consultant. This suggestion arose during an initial discussion between Dr. Duhl and Dean Baker:

DR. DUHL: Can I ask a question? I'm not in the business world and maybe I should turn to the Dean to ask this. There have been many corporations in crisis in much the same way our cities are. The money is there but something has gone wrong with their mechanisms. The mechanisms don't keep tuned up to the time. They've lost touch with certain parts of the operation. What sort of consultant has been the best kind of help for a corporation in that kind of position? And is there any parallel between that kind of help and the kind of help the cities should receive to deal with the same kind of issues?

DEAN BAKER: I should think there are a lot of common factors. Getting something done in a corporation requires real dissatisfaction on the part of those outside of management who have a vital interest. They're likely to fire the management or take out of management hands the responsibility for solving the problem. New management people coming in, or the group who are dissatisfied, are quite likely to use consultants to determine what needs to be done.

I wonder, listening to this, why it takes any different approach from that which was followed in Pittsburgh. I don't think that what happened in Pittsburgh came to Mr. Mellon one night between three and four in the morning when he was lying awake. I gather there were three or four people who, discussing the problems of Pittsburgh, became concerned about it and went to him and found, as a community leader, that he was interested and responded well to their idea of what should be done. And from that point on, whether you work with a committee or whether you hire consultants depends upon the breadth of view and the ability of that particular group.

One group of consultants received particular attention—the systems analysts. Dean Baker pointed to the businessmen's experience with this new approach, and it was learned that Mayor Cavanagh has been experimenting along the same lines in Detroit.

DEAN BAKER: I think there is one other thing businessmen can offer. It seems to me that some businessmen in fairly big industries have had experience with what's called "systems analysis." They don't understand it and they're a little opposed to it, but nevertheless, in this day and age, you do have firms that specialize in this.

Sometimes it seems to me as though systems analysis is based primarily on the idea that you take people who know nothing about the situation, and they somehow have an advantage. But it isn't really that. It's that they look at the whole picture. You don't look at the police force or one or two things. You look at the whole thing. There are techniques for that.

There are businessmen who have used these techniques and who have done studies of their industries. They are in touch with university people, and they are in touch with other businessmen who have been exposed to that type of thinking. They can bring into a group that is getting excited and wants to do something about a city a little of their background. I don't think many politicians or ministers normally get any chance to have contact with systems analysis.

DR. DUHL: As an aside, it is very interesting that very early Jerry Cavanagh linked up with Wayne University, where he made contact with these systems people. He's been working on this now for three years. He picked this up from something that came from Ford. The point is, he's made just the linkage that you're talking about.

The search for a mechanism led also to the Demonstration Cities Bill, described in the chapter on housing and urban renewal. A businessman was afraid that it would amount to another housing program, merely amplifying all the pitfalls of previous housing programs. Dr. Duhl explained that this was not the case. Another businessman saw further possibilities for the systems analysis approach within the structure of the Bill itself:

BUSINESSMAN: I don't know enough about this Demonstration Cities concept, but it seems to me that it's essentially a housing approach. I must say that unless it is a total concept, and includes such things as employment and a host of other things, I don't see how you can ever come out of something like that and feel that you've proved anything. Sure, you can prove that for a given expenditure of money, things are somewhat better. But if the idea is to prove what can be done with a given number of people or a given area, I don't quite see how.

You ask the question: how would a business run it? A business that is test marketing an idea is seeking to establish that, with a given expenditure of money, you can accomplish certain things.

Is this Demonstration Cities thing designed to use a practical sum of money for a given number of people to accomplish a stated objective in total?

DR. DUHL: Let me try to summarize it. I think there was just a wee bit of confusion this morning. The Demonstration Cities approach will focus on a pilot area of a community which contains approximately 10% of the population. It's usually the area with the greatest amount of substandard housing. These are the same areas that the President's Committee on Delinquency has been concerned with, the poverty people have been concerned with, and so forth. Now, for the first time, what we are saying is: any local community that can add up all the federal funding that goes into that area—all the various separate packages—and can find some mechanism of tying it together, including health, education, welfare, poverty programs, urban renewal, housing, you name it—we'll give 80% of your local contribution as free money. In a sense, this is the first attempt to give the city money for a wholistic-type planning across the board. In other words, you can use all the existing resources. You can use the Labor Department's offices to find jobs. You can use manpower training. But this is additional money for coordination purposes.

We keep asking: what is the problem in the community? One of the things that strikes me is that mechanisms through which the police chief, the poverty people, and the health and welfare people can sit down and get together and talk just don't exist. We have hardly been able to get these various groups together, in city after city. I'm saying "we" in a generic sense—not the federal government.

But suppose we were able to establish mechanisms like this on the local level for first-hand communication. Suppose a city, in order to become effective, for the first time collected data which, instead of being health data and education data, become data which get integrated. Suppose the mayor's office (and this is what Cavanagh has in Detroit) has the ability to evaluate all of the data coming in, and begins to make choices about what the priorities should be. This gets to be a competent city.

The whole goal of the Demonstration Cities Program is to give enough money to start on a small area in the community. Ultimately, as the Secretary indicated, there is probably going to be much more federal money going into the cities. The cities will begin to expand these mechanisms, so that they can do some planning for the whole area.

BUSINESSMAN: There's a precedent for what you're talking about in other places. It's being done in business today. That is the establishment of a system which is, of course, people, methods and machines. Our space agency has developed a system to go to the moon, which is made up of men, methods and machines. Communities just now are beginning to look at transportation systems, rather than the highway system and the public transportation system. It seems to me that we are beginning to see now some concern in the community for, if you want, a people system, which is the structure within these communities. These systems overlap with one another, but they are about the only way that I've seen to break through the traditional fragmentations. You establish fragmentations, but at least they're much bigger ones that you can look at in total.

Timing

A familiar thread ran throughout the social problems discussion. It was pointed out that nothing was likely to happen until things really got bad. This is the same theme that cropped up in the discussion on transportation. It appeared this time in a discussion on how to get started:

DEAN BAKER: I should think, as far as getting started is concerned, once you had a group of people—it can be a small group —who can excite some of the people that are thought highly of in the city, then the next step, which is the study in depth of the problem on a broad scale, wouldn't be too hard to get going.

DR. DUHL: I think you're right. I think you put your finger on one issue, and that is: they were hurting in Pittsburgh.

DEAN BAKER: Absolutely. Until they were hurting, nothing happened. I don't think it ever does. You've got to have people become concerned. Perhaps this really means that the essential thing is to have done the thinking beforehand, and then you just have to wait for a sequence of events whereby a community becomes really aroused and unhappy. Then be ready to move in with the suggestions, rather than trying to force a solution when it won't take.

DR. DUHL: I've been to about 40 or 50 different cities around the country, and I'd say that in the bulk of them you'll find a few people who are hurting. But the ordinary citizen, the ordinary businessman, the ordinary professional—the doctor—he's not hurting. He doesn't really see what anybody's talking about when we talk about a crisis in the cities: "The poor—they belong over there. Transportation—I got my own car. I can always go any place I want to." I must say there are really very few cities that I've gone to where the city as a whole, or the key leadership in the city, say: "We're hurting and we've got to do something about it."

Some Examples

Dr. Duhl's conjecture is supported by the paucity of examples of action, not to mention effective action. It was intimated above that Pittsburgh has made some progress, but that it was mostly of the brick-and-mortar type. A careful reading of Robert Pease's remarks during the discussion on housing and urban renewal reveals that Pittsburgh, with the support of business, is moving into the social aspects of rebuilding the city. As noted in the background paper, Pittsburgh's ACTION-Housing, Inc., a business-supported organization, represents a step in the same direction.

There was some discussion of the experience in Boston following the West End misfortune:

BUSINESSMAN: I was thinking of Boston. You know, it's quite different from Pittsburgh and Detroit. In one sense it's over-organized with no organization. So where would you make a dent? Where would you get something started? How would you approach a city such as Boston?

DEAN BAKER: I suppose you would build on the cooperation which has developed between [Mayor] Collins and some business groups and other groups in getting the new buildings built. That took an amount of coordination and cooperation that we'd never seen before.

BUSINESSMAN: Prudential came in and nothing happened until Prudential said to the city: "We're going to move. We're going to leave." All of a sudden a group mobilized to deal with that particular crisis and then it disappeared.

The most powerful man, and thank goodness he's an enlightened individual, is the Cardinal. When anything needs to be done in the city, people run to the Cardinal. He does want the city to move forward, so he suddenly gets to work behind the Stadium Authority, and behind this, that and the other thing. But the businessmen as a group don't seem to have any real resources of their own.

DEAN BAKER: I think it comes back to the fact that everybody thought and prognosticated that Boston was going to go to hell. It's doing so well now that I don't think most people think there's any emergency at the moment. Emergencies often arise very quickly, and we are not ready for them. Maybe we could organize a private planning group that was concerned and that would be worried about slowly moving toward being ready when we got in some kind of a jam.

Dr. Duhl had a few recommendations for today's large, urban centers:

There are a series of problems in big cities which could be handled by areas within the city. You could break the city down into smaller areas and begin to talk about education, police, and welfare in terms of areas that are handleable. Now, there are certain things that can't be done that way—like transportation, streets, water, and things like that. But we can start by talking about the police, and schools, about welfare, and health for areas of three or four hundred thousand that might be handleable.

You already have area-wide planning councils in New York; but they are dealing with physical planning in the city. These planning councils could be expanded so that they might become concerned with much more than just the physical buildings.

SUMMARY

By and large, the history of social problems and attempts to deal with them is not encouraging. The gap still seems very large. The discussion revealed quite clearly that until mechanisms are found by which business leaders and other community leaders can come in contact with and understand social problems, it makes little sense to talk about the exact nature of the businessman's role. No one knows what a good solution to the problem of the slums looks like. No one knows the costs and no one has accurately and concretely assessed the benefits.

If there is a recommendation to the businessman, then, it is that he become involved. He is in a better position than most to experiment with the use of boards and consultants and new management techniques in the formulation and implementation of policy. Let him experiment and observe the results before he passes judgment as to whether or not this is an area of proper concern and of action, and before the community passes judgment as to whether or not it wishes to encourage business participation.

Selected Bibliography

Beshers, James M. *Urban Social Structure* (New York: Free Press, 1962).

Chamber of Commerce of the USA. *Concept of Poverty* (Washington: 1965).

Duhl, L. J. *The Urban Condition: People and Policy* (New York: Basic Books, 1963).

Gist, Noel P. and Silvia Fava. *Urban Society,* 5th ed. (New York: Crowell, 1964).

Harrington, Michael. *The Other America* (Baltimore: Penguin Books, 1962).

Johnson, Elmer H. *Crime, Correction, and Society* (Homewood, Ill.: Dorsey, 1964).

Krosney, H. *Beyond Welfare: Poverty in the Supercity* (New York: Holt, Rinehart & Winston, 1966).

Lomas, G. M., ed. *Social Aspects of Urban Development* (London: National Council of Social Service, 1966).

Seligman, Benjamin B. *Poverty as a Public Issue* (New York: Free Press, 1965).

Weaver, Robert C. *Dilemmas of Urban America* (Cambridge: Harvard University Press, 1965). (Godkin Lectures, 1965.)

CHAPTER VIII

Air and Water Pollution

The discussion on air and water pollution had, within the framework of this conference, two outstanding properties. First, the issues which arose—how to set and enforce standards to achieve social benefits, and how to share the cost of meeting these standards—were in unusually sharp focus. Second, the pollution control problem did not appear to be closely interrelated with other urban problems. This independence permitted the participants to reach a few tentative conclusions. Since the issues are, or are likely to become, central issues as other urban problems become more clearly defined, the conclusions which were reached deserve special attention.

The session began with brief statements by Secretary of the Interior Stewart Udall regarding water and Thomas Williams, Information Officer of the Public Health Service's Division of Air Pollution Control, regarding air. Both men assumed that the participants had read the background paper. The paper will, therefore, precede the opening statements.

The general discussion which followed the opening remarks did not adhere rigidly to the structure of the background paper. Since most of the topics raised in the paper were discussed at one point or another, however, the paper's structure will be used as a guide in outlining the discussion.

Background Paper

According to some sources, almost every creek, river, lake, and bay in the United States is seriously contaminated and despoiled.

According to others, a five- or six-day stationary weather front coupled with a temperature inversion would turn most United States cities into gas chambers. Fortunately, this has not yet happened. It almost happened in New York in October 1963, and was averted only by a cold air mass on the fifth day. It almost happened in New York in 1953, allegedly causing some 200 deaths.

Both air and water pollution are reasonably well understood. We know the sources, and we know how to detect the conditions. To a great extent, we know how to prevent, or at least curtail, most types of pollution. There is only one basic difficulty. Pollution control is extremely expensive if the total burden for control is placed on the polluters.

The afternoon discussion group on May 20 will focus on the problems of how to set reasonable standards and how to share the cost of meeting them. As preparation for that discussion, this paper will first present some background data on the scope of the problem. It will then identify the groups concerned with pollution, and will suggest some issues which arise out of the divergent interests of these groups. Finally, it will offer some possible courses of action which might be evaluated and augmented as the discussion proceeds.

INTRODUCTION

For a long time pollution was not a problem. Water regenerates itself naturally, given that there is enough water and a sufficient distance between sources of pollution. Air currents remove smog naturally, given that there is not too much. What has happened, of course, is that water use and air use have increased to the point of saturation in many areas, most of them urban. Looking at water, for example, in 1900 there were 90 bgd (billions of gallons per day) of usable water available and only 40 bgd used. In 1960 there were 320 bgd available and used. It is estimated that by 1980 with current water control practices, there will be 520 bgd available and 600 bgd demanded. The United States Chamber of Commerce has estimated water consumption by the three principal water users over the same period:

	1900	*1960*	*1980*
Industry	38%	50%	66%
Municipalities	7%	7%	6%
Irrigation	55%	43%	28%

In other words, not only will demand outstrip supply, but the per cent of use by industry, a major source of pollution, particularly in urban areas, will rise significantly.

The seriousness of the air pollution problem is less easily documented because it depends so heavily upon weather conditions and terrain. A Senate committee has estimated, however, that 308 urban areas, containing a quarter of our population, have a major air pollution problem. Of the areas with populations greater than 500,000, 75% have a major air pollution problem.

The benefits which would accrue from reduced pollution of either type are not easily quantified. There would be more fish, more oysters, more weekend boaters, cleaner buildings and trees, and maybe healthier and happier people. President Kennedy estimated in 1963 that the *annual* property damage due to air pollution alone was $11 billion, or $65 per United States citizen. While such estimates must be subjected to careful scrutiny, especially when made in conjunction with annual health program messages, they give some indication of the magnitude of the problem.

The cost side is not much clearer. There are some estimates. Presently about one-fourth of our towns and cities have no sewage-treatment plants of any kind, and half of the existing plants are outdated. To bring municipalities up-to-date would cost an estimated $40 billion. This includes no industrial costs, which, for competitive reasons, are more difficult to come by. One estimate puts the current total industry investment in equipment for water pollution control at $1 billion and the annual operating expense of that equipment at $100 million. In contrast, the steel industry estimates that if it alone had to meet the water standards recommended by the Public Health Service, the annual cost in 1965 would have been $260 million, or about one-quarter of its net earnings. Likewise, the chemical industry estimates that it now builds $50 million worth of water pollution control facilities a year and spends $40 million a year to operate control equipment.

On the air side, a recent article in *Fortune* tabulates the *annual* cost of proper control as follows:

Industry	$1.00 billion
Automobiles	.80 billion
Utilities	.60 billion
Rubbish disposal	.35 billion
Miscellaneous other	.25 billion
	$3.00 billion

While these costs compare favorably with the $11 billion annual loss due to air pollution, the $3 billion figure is not universally agreed upon. One industrial witness at a Senate hearing, for example, estimated an annual cost of $50-$75 billion for industry alone if air pollution were to be fully controlled.

The estimates vary widely because the estimators are talking about different levels of control and purity. In the case of water, the cost depends heavily on the purity of the water. If a steel plant has to return drinking water to a river, the cost will be very high. The *Fortune* estimates for air pollution control are based on the goal of removing two-thirds of the total pollution. No reference is made to the fact that the remaining one-third may be concentrated in a few areas where it would be extremely expensive to achieve a desirable atmosphere.

The other point, of course, is that even if the annual cost of pollution control were $3 billion and the benefits were $11 billion, the people who would benefit would not necessarily be the people who are asked to pay. This brings us to the interest groups.

THE INTEREST GROUPS

Since the groups who take an interest in water pollution are somewhat different from those interested in the atmosphere, the two will be discussed separately.

Water

Perhaps the most obvious groups are the aroused citizens in each community threatened by pollution—the angry men like David Blaushild in Cleveland, who took his young daughter to his child-hood swimming hole and, finding it polluted, began to wage his own private war, with Lake Erie as the primary target. There are groups like the one at Lake Tahoe, who see their gold mine turning into a sewer. There are the drinkers of water in New York who cannot tap the Hudson in time of drought because it is polluted. There are the residents of Pittsburgh, or Cambridge, or Washington, who simply cannot stand the smell. All of these groups tend to become extremist, with the attitude: "Pollution is wrong and we must stop it."

There is another group which is equally extreme but more specific: the conservationists. They want to see fish in the rivers and trees on the banks, and, in general, they have a good idea of what is killing the fish.

The result of citizen displeasure has, in many cases, been the formation of local, regional, or state pollution control boards which set standards and, in some cases, have limited enforcement powers. The effectiveness of these local government bodies depends quite heavily on the cooperation of another major interest group: the polluters. If the polluters see that it is in their best interest, for public relations reasons, to curtail pollution, then the control board will appear effective. If, on the other hand, a large company does not want to cooperate, it can resist with remarkably little effort. It can threaten to leave the area, for example, or to work actively to have the local control officials replaced.

Realizing that the success of local regulation was situational, but not wanting to usurp local powers if that could be avoided, the United States Congress passed the Water Quality Act of 1965. This Act gives the states until June 30, 1967, to set standards which must be approved by the Federal Water Pollution Control Administration (FWPCA). If no standards have been set, the state governor can apply for and receive a 6-month moratorium.

This approach has the effect of making it increasingly difficult for the states to avoid setting standards while giving them an interim period to take action. As far as polluters are concerned, it means that the risk of being taken to court will increase over time, but that there still remains an opportunity to work with local pollution control boards to find a reasonable compromise.

A final group which stands to benefit from increased pollution control, no matter who pays for it, is the manufacturers of pollution control equipment. Potentially, this is a large and expanding group. The Nalco Chemical Company, a specialist in water pollution control, is a good example of a firm which has entered the field. The recent activity in Nalco's stock reflects the financial community's interest in the future of the industry.

Air

As with water, aroused citizens are an important group when the air gets bad enough. Again, their position is an extreme one. They search desperately for economic or medical criteria to back up their anger. Their evidence is sketchy. President Kennedy's $11 billion annual loss estimate is certainly subject to debate, and no medical source is willing to admit a positive connection between pollution and disease. Former Surgeon General Luther Terry will say that "there is no longer any doubt that air pollution is a hazard to health." He neglects to mention that hot, humid weather and thin ice are also health hazards.

Given the lack of direct evidence that air pollution is anything more than an inconvenience, it is not surprising that the air polluters as a class have been able to hold out against the regulators with more success than the water polluters, the one exception being the drivers of automobiles. By federal law, the Secretary of Health, Education, and Welfare is authorized to establish and enforce automotive emission standards by 1968. Aside from the automotive field, the setting of standards and the enforcement of these standards by a government body, be it local, regional, state, or federal, have been extremely sparse. The only notable exception is in California, where state laws have already set automotive exhaust standards, and city regulations in Los Angeles have affected trash incineration and stack discharge by local power and industrial companies. The federal government may be asked by a state governor for help in intrastate abatement proceedings, but can assume no initiative on its own unless there is positive evidence of interstate pollution. Even then, the most that the Secretary of HEW can do is request the United States Attorney General to bring suit to secure abatement.

If the federal government were able to demonstrate that the cost of stopping or curtailing either air or water pollution were far less than the benefits gained, there would still be hesitancy to act, for there remains the basic issue: Who is to pay?

THE ISSUES

The basic issue of who is to pay can be usefully subdivided into several subsidiary issues. Since the problem for both air and water pollution is roughly the same, they will be treated together.

The first subissue is simply: What is an acceptable environment? The aroused proponents of pollution control practically refuse to argue this question. To admit that something less than pure air or pure water is acceptable is to drop back into a debate which, in their minds, is strictly a delaying tactic on the part of the polluters. David Blaushild of Cleveland represents this group clearly when he says: "Our so-called leaders remain pathetically unimpelled. Unless immediate action is taken, without more surveys or lengthy debates about who is responsible or where the money is coming from, then Lake Erie is doomed. In my opinion, it should be declared a disaster area. Then we might get action that will catch up with the pollution."

If the debate is read carefully, however, it is discovered that different water users require different levels of water purity and that higher levels of purity tend to be far more expensive to obtain. Similarly, greater air purity can be obtained at increasing cost. Unfortunately, no one seems willing or able to draw up the curves for each city which reveal the tradeoffs. The aroused citizens fear a compromise which will leave them without swimming holes and clean air, and industry, which has been remarkably successful at avoiding regulation, has been hesitant to generate data which would help the government in setting standards. Now that federal standards are to be imposed, however, the issue must come out in the open. There is a real danger that unless it develops alternative standards and justifies them on a cost basis, industry may be forced to produce mountain air and spring water. What are reasonable standards? Should it be necessary that a citizen be able to catch a fish in every stream? Is it reasonable, much less good business, to insist on clean air? Businessmen in Pittsburgh said that it was. Others have not.

Quite apart from the question of standards and degree is the question of whether or not the total cost of industrial pollution control should be borne by industry. It is not surprising to find James Quigley, Assistant Secretary of HEW and acting commissioner of the FWPCA, saying, "No one has the *right* to use America's rivers as a sewer" and, "You must accept the principle that the cost of pollution control from now on is part of the cost of doing business." On the same day, Governor Henry Bellman of Oklahoma said that the "assimilation of wastes is unavoidably one of the multipurpose uses that water must serve, and this must be recognized by all concerned."

The argument in favor of forcing business to bear the total cost of pollution control frequently ignores one fundamental aspect of the private enterprise economy: The increased cost will be passed on to the consumer. This raises at least two issues. First, because some polluters in the same industry are more favorably located from a pollution standpoint than others, the cost of meeting national pollution standards will be greater to some than others. To the extent that these companies compete in the same market, the setting and enforcing of standards clearly discriminates against the less favorably located companies. Is this the intention of FWPCA? Second, will the inevitable price rise be acceptable to the President's economic advisors during an inflationary period, and, if not, how is investment in pollution control equipment to be tied to the other aspects of fiscal policy?

It can be argued that the real problem is not pollution as such but the increasing density of the urban community, and that the cost of controlling pollution should be borne by the community. How should this be done? Since it is a regional problem with regional benefits, the use of federal funds seems inappropriate. Is it realistic to ask a regional government to float a bond issue to build and operate pollution control equipment for a particular plant, particularly when such equipment allows the owner to use more efficient fuels and make a greater profit?

If it is insisted that the federal government must share the expense of control, what mechanisms are to be used? The Internal Revenue Service shies away from special tax advantages because it feels ill at ease trying to separate public benefit from private gain, particularly in the air pollution field. Direct grants may well raise the same discrimination arguments associated with a regional bond issue. Who, then, is to pay, and how?

However this question is answered, there is a third, perhaps more bewildering issue. Who is to set and enforce standards? This will probably be determined for both air and water in the next five years. It will definitely be determined for water by 1968. From the businessman's point of view, there may be a number of advantages to local regulation. There may be more room for negotiation and influence. The businessman can threaten to leave. Also, by working with a local agency, the businessman can sometimes arrange to keep effluent data confidential. This may be important in certain industries where such data is of value to competitors; confidential data is not in keeping with federal standard-setting procedures.

From another standpoint, the federally established and enforced standard may be more equitable. It puts the small company which may not be in an influential position in its local region on an equal footing with a large company in the same region. Likewise, it puts similar firms in different regions on the same footing.

The process of setting standards and the determination of who is to pay to meet these standards raise unpleasant issues which will not be resolved easily. On the other hand, if business does not take part in their resolution, they will probably be resolved without business participation, and not necessarily to business' best advantage.

POSSIBLE COURSES OF ACTION

Objectives

There are essentially two positions which a business can take with respect to pollution control costs. At one end, outlays for pollution control may be viewed as expenditures with zero return, in which case the object will be to minimize such expenditures over time. At the other extreme, business may view the environment in which it lives as a critical factor in determining its future success. Clean air and/or clean water may be regarded as essential in drawing customers or holding a work force. In that case, expenditures on pollution control equipment are not zero-return expenditures, and the object is to determine that level of expenditure over time which will maximize the firm's future success.

Alternative Strategies

If the object of minimum expenditures is chosen, there are a number of alternative strategies available. First, a businessman can do nothing in the hope that by the time he is forced to do something, researchers will have discovered new technologies which will lower the cost of control significantly or that federal grants and incentives for control will be greatly increased.

Alternatively he might get together with other businessmen in the area and work out a compromise with the local regulatory body. If such an agency does not exist, he might encourage the establishment of one. In the compromise with this agency, it might be possible to define an acceptable level of pollution over time and a schedule of improvements to meet the target. By taking this voluntary action the businessman is much more likely to be last rather than first on the federal government's list of offenders. This will buy him time, and perhaps give him a competitive advantage over the company which is doing nothing.

If, as a polluter or a nonpolluter, a businessman feels that the environment will be important to the future of his city, and he wants to take the initiative in cleaning it up, he can proceed in a number of ways. Pittsburgh solved its smoke problem by gathering local business leaders together and agreeing that, despite the $275 million it would cost, industrial smoke had to be stopped. It then worked with local government to get a city ordinance passed which prohibited the burning of soft coal anywhere in the city. The same type of thing has been done in Los Angeles with the power companies and the trash burners.

In the case of water pollution, the alternatives depend very much on the situation. If polluters are isolated and upstream of the

city, they may have to act on their own. In the immediate vicinity
of the city, however, there are a number of ways of working with
the city to solve the problem. For example, if there is a large company in a relatively small city the company can work with the city
on a municipal sewer system for which it pays user charges to cover
operating expenses. In this way, the city builds and benefits from
the facility and the company expenses its water pollution control
efforts, with a considerable tax advantage. Also, if the sewer is
well planned and designed, the city is eligible for a federal construction grant of 30% of the cost or $1.2 million, whichever is
smaller.[1] In a city like Atlanta, which must spend at a minimum
$100 million to update its facilities, this federal money is not
significant. In a smaller city, it may be.

In a relatively large city, a company might install a primary
pollution control system which removed those wastes which the
city system was not designed to handle, tying this primary system
to the city system on a user-charge basis. Again, most of the advantages of working with the city would accrue and, incidentally,
the enforcing agency would deal with the city, not the company.

Finally, considering the fact that pollution control legislation is
still in its formative stages, it may be in business' best interest to
step up its lobbying activities in Washington. A well-informed
lobbyist could go a long way toward substituting fact for fiction,
and, in the process, encourage the Congress to consider some form
of tax relief or a more reasonable limit to the size of federal grants.

SUMMARY

It is not expected that in two hours you will be able to cover
all of the issues raised in this brief paper. In all likelihood, as you
bring your experience to bear on the problems, additional issues
will be generated. Our intention, however, is to have the discussion
extend beyond issues. The object of the conference is to develop
clearly defined courses of action for you, as business leaders, to
consider. You may not reach a consensus as to which course of

---

[1] Since the paper was first written, the availability of federal grants has
greatly increased, making the joint industry-community approach more
attractive. See also footnote [3].

action is best, but it is hoped that you will go away knowing the implications of each alternative for you, your firm, and your urban area.

Discussion

INTRODUCTORY REMARKS BY SECRETARY UDALL

One needn't rehearse the history of air pollution and water pollution in this country. I think that it is inevitable that people will take resources for granted, as we have done in so many areas of our national life, until it becomes apparent, through the over-presence of wastes, that we have gone down the wrong road and must reverse our policies.

I think the question, in both air and water pollution, that the country faces today and has not resolved is: how do you organize in order to solve these problems permanently? What in terms of new governmental institutions do we need? What is the proper pattern of contribution by the federal government, the state government, and the local governments? What about industry and its role in air and water pollution abatement, which is so vital because the wastes of industry are a major part of the problem. What is reasonable and equitable and expectable in terms of industry? Ultimately we get down, of course, to political and economic questions which are intermingled, it seems to me, with the solution of the basic organizational problem.

I'd like to give you a little bit of our current thinking. I am going to talk about water because this is where I've had to concentrate my own energies. I'll leave my commissioner [James Quigley] here. He is thoroughly familiar with, and in fact I think we share the same views on, most of the major issues.

The problem the country confronts in terms of water pollution today is that we are not presently organized. We don't have a systematic approach to cleaning up rivers. We haven't developed standards for water pollution, although we shall in the next fifteen months.

A week ago we sent out to the governors our guidelines for the standards that are to be developed under the Water Quality Act the President signed last October. The states will have until July 1 of next year to make their determinations and submit them to us. So we're really on the edge of what will be a very interesting period in terms of water management in this country. I think we are going to determine largely during the next two or three years what institutions and mechanisms and economic principles the country is going to adopt in terms of tackling this very big problem.

The very basis of the President's Clean Rivers Bill, submitted this year, was the fact that the federal government conceded the point for the first time, in terms of its own economics, that it should make a major contribution towards tackling and licking this big national problem. It is proposed in the legislation, providing certain conditions were met—that we organize in the right way politically with an effective pattern of cooperation—that the federal government would make grants to the extent of 30% of the total cost. This would be, of course, not to industry, but to municipalities. Some have suggested that this figure should be higher. It will not surprise us if Congress raises the figure to 40%.

Indeed, the one state that has, I think, had the boldest and most forward looking leadership in the last year is the State of New York. The [state] legislature unanimously passed a billion dollar bond issue designed to clean up New York's rivers. The people of New York voted four to one for that bond issue, which was, we think, a resounding expression of public opinion. New York now is ready to go. One of Governor Rockefeller's premises was that the state should put up 30%, the federal government should put up 30%, and the local communities should put up 40% of the total. He suggested this as a pattern. It is something like this that is probably going to emerge.

You then have a further problem to which the President's Bill addresses itself. We are not, if we are wise stewards of our resources, and if we really want to have a clean country, interested in cleaning up the current backlog. We're interested in keeping our rivers clean—in managing our water in ways that we don't manage it at the present time—in a very systematic way with set standards that we all adhere to.

The issue in that regard is: How should we organize? What is the proper method of organization in terms of water as a resource?

It is very obvious to us that you have to observe the nature of water. Water falls on a watershed. It exists in a river basin. The people in that basin share it as a common resource. We are tending to move water between basins and we will do a lot more of that in years ahead, there is no doubt. But in the main, the river basin is where nature puts water. Unless we have everybody that shares a particular river, large or small, working on a common program, you can't expect, as an end result, to carry on a clean-up program and to be organized in such a way politically that you can keep a river clean and manage your water properly.

We saw recently a most interesting river program—one that they have in the Ruhr Valley in Germany—regarding water quality management. Here you have an intense concentration of industry on two, what we would call small, rivers, and the water is literally passed down from factory to factory and from community to community. It has to be managed, and they've had organizations there for 60 years. They are much like western irrigation districts, or much like districts that we have for water management in some parts of our country, where everybody works together for a common objective. This is one of the reasons we feel that the big problem today is to get organized so that we have political institutions that can function.

Then you run into the next question: should the whole thing be run from Washington, or where should it be run? Although we think it's important to have national standards, or at least to have standards that are nationally administered, and to have national enforcement powers, it's our view that water, particularly on the enforcement side, should be handled much like law enforcement. If you can get people who are neighbors sharing a particular river or resource to run their own program, this is the most effective way to do it. And, of course, we now have a test of whether the states are going to provide strong leadership along the lines of New York and other states that I could mention, and really get into the business of making substantial grants themselves and of helping out. This is, again, an important part of the problem.

Let me discuss the industry aspect a moment because this is one that many of you around the table are quite properly interested in.

This aspect of it is discussed very intelligently in the [background] paper. I don't think anyone is proposing, in regard to industry, that the federal government should make grants to industry. There have been various proposals, and you may want to discuss some of them here today. To me there are certainly a lot of strong pros and cons with regard to the various tax incentives which might be provided. After all, a water pollution abatement facility is not, in a strict sense, economic. It's serving a social purpose primarily, and one can make the argument that, therefore, this is a classic case for tax incentive of some kind. It was interesting in the State of New York, for example, that they provided, by state law, that such facilities are not subject to real estate tax, which certainly seems to make a great deal of sense. Some communities provide that such facilities are not subject to a use tax.

The suggestion in this [background] paper is one that many industries are already following—of making contracts with local communities, where it is possible to have large facilities built that combine municipal and industrial wastes. Sometimes this isn't possible; sometimes it is. And of course you get economies of scale. Thus industry can, if it wants to, contract for payments rather than building its own facilities, and thereby write it off as part of the cost of doing business.

My own view on a larger issue of standards, for what it's worth, is that one can make out a very strong case for having national standards in this field. I am a believer in the fact that, when we get to enforcement and to carrying out programs, the more local it is the better, providing you get a sound program to begin with. We're already confronted with a situation in many areas of the country where people are in the same business but in different states, and one state has a set of standards that requires a high degree of costly treatment and another one does not. This may penalize industry. It may cause industry to consider locating in other parts of the country, either where there is more water or lower standards. We find, even with the existing legislation, that under this double standard we have set up, navigable rivers may end up having one set of standards and nonnavigable rivers another. Two pulp mills, for example, in the same state might have a different set of standards, thereby producing economic dislocations. I'm a strong believer in putting industry on an equal footing if possible. To that extent, national standards, or at least standards that do not have wide disparities in different regions of the country, are quite important.

It is also obvious as an economic consideration that, if we are going to have a national clean water program, the major portion of the cost of it is going to be passed right on to the consumer. The consumer might as well face that as a fact. I think that the New York vote and other things we see all over the country are an indication that people are ready and willing to bear the cost—that they will pay the price of a clean-up program.

There are many considerations that are involved here. Some of us who have been quite close to this program feel that industry has, in the main, had a change of heart on this in the last few years. I think it is in part because leadership in some segments of industry has shown that really it wasn't as costly and wasn't as difficult as others had thought. Some industries have demonstrated that by cooperating with local people—by gearing into municipal systems—economies can be achieved and, again, it isn't as burdensome as it was thought to be.

Another reason, I think, is an awareness that there is a public demand for action. It always pleases me to see business concerns in this country do a good job in terms of conservation of resources. I have watched many of them do some very excellent things. I have seen many of them weave it right into their institutional advertising—showing what they are doing to help conserve natural resources and to conserve the environment. Many of them can see this more and more—particularly if they are on equal footing with other people—as an opportunity to be a good citizen and do their part and to get due credit from the public for it.

As you can tell from this brief presentation, we have a problem. We are all wrestling with it; all of us here at the table are involved in it. I don't think we are organized properly at this point to lick the problem. I think we face a crucial period of action. Some have said, speaking of our nation's largest city, that it's ungovernable. I don't believe that for a minute. I just happen to think that it is ill-organized. I think it's ill-organized in many ways. You have to organize to manage your water and your air and your transportation, and this has been a large area of national failure. The question that the President has asked in his message is: Does a country that is as prosperous and as affluent and as technically capable as we are have the capacity to be both a wealthy country and a clean country as well? I think this is the larger challenge that we face.

INTRODUCTORY REMARKS BY THOMAS WILLIAMS

Much of the general outline that Secretary Udall presented for water pollution applies to air also. As you know, the problem is caused, by and large, by the same forces of growth and urbanization that make for the water pollution problem. I think, in general, in air pollution we are a bit behind the water pollution control people in our approach. However, I would say, starting in about 1963, when the Clean Air Act was passed, we began to make a significant attempt to do something about the air pollution problem.

As you may recall, the Clean Air Act, signed by President Johnson in December of 1963, for the first time gave the federal government authority to give matching grants for the improvement or establishment of state and local air pollution control programs and provided for federal abatement action similar to that which had been in force for some years in interstate water problems. In 1965 the Clean Air Act amendments were passed. They provide direct federal authority to control auto emissions by means of federal standards. These have been implemented and will be in effect, as most of you know, in the 1968 model year.

In general, the response by state and local governments to the financial stimulation of the Clean Air Act has been very good. We've had a 50% increase in the budgets now available for state and local governments for control programs. But a 50% increase of a very inadequate amount is still a very inadequate amount.

By and large, air pollution control at the state and local levels of government is obsolete. It is run by people who are still thinking in terms of smoke abatement which, as you know, reached its heyday in our country in the late '40s. Smoke abatement standards by no means constitute what today would be considered adequate air pollution control practices, whether for industry or for the public and others who have to enjoy or not enjoy the air.

I believe, paralleling what Secretary Udall said about water, as far as we see it in the [air pollution] program, industry's response to the problem of air pollution has taken a decided turn for the better in the last five or six years. I can recall when it seemed to me that the usual response by industrial spokesmen to air pollution was to say: "Forget about it. If you can't see it and you can't smell it too much, forget about it. It isn't really there." I don't believe that is true any more. As I remarked to an audience of school administrators earlier this week, sometimes it is quite apparent to me that in the last few years, especially among larger industries, the attitude toward air pollution is more enlightened, here again from our point of view, than is the attitude of some, or a great number actually, of state and local authorities dealing with the problem in a direct legislative fashion.

DEFINING AN ACCEPTABLE ENVIRONMENT

One of the accomplishments of the general discussion was to establish firmly the principle that there is no such thing as "the acceptable environment" for either air or water. It was evident that many businessmen came to the meeting with the assumption that imposing standards meant imposing a single standard. As one businessman put it:

> If Republic [Steel Co.] gets the air dirty, or some other company gets it dirty, they've got to clean it up before they put it back. There is no argument about that. You can't have somebody come in from the outside and set standards which are perfectly arbitrary. There is only one standard for water and for air—and that's clean.

Commissioner Quigley assured the group that the Department of the Interior had no intention of setting a single standard:

> There is a need, as Secretary Udall pointed out, for national standards. I would hasten to add that this does not mean uniform standards. We are not trying to set the same standards of quality on all of the interstate waters of this country. I think this would be a totally pie-in-the-sky, completely unrealistic approach. We

recognize that the quality of water that flows in the various inter-state streams varies markedly.

In substance, just hitting the highlights of these guidelines,[2] I think they make clear to the states that we expect that whatever standards they set will definitely hold the line—that waters will not be permitted to get any dirtier or any more polluted than they presently are. In other words, the present situation is the floor below which we hope they will not go, directly or indirectly.

The second point that the guidelines make clear, as does the Act itself, is that the purpose of the guidelines is to enhance the quality of the water in the streams. It is not to lock in any present pollution, neither is it designed to lock out any possible future use. I think we recognize that industry is going to have to grow, and industry is going to have to develop. There are going to be some subsequent pollution problems. But I think what we are trying to do through the standards approach is to lay out what we hope the quality of the water in a river will become, say, over a five-year period.

I think what we're trying to get at in the Clean Rivers approach (which is embodied in the Administration's Bill[3]) is to move toward the new concepts and the new organizations that Secretary Udall referred to as essential if we are honestly going to do a capable, conscientious, organized job of managing our rivers. The Delaware River Basin approach is, we think, the forerunner of the pattern that is likely to be developed and followed in many of our river basins in the future, and this is what the Clean Rivers [Bill] is designed to get at. Now, whether it passes or not and whether it becomes operative or not, the requirement for water quality standards is on the books, and the standards will have to be submitted sometime within the next year.

Mr. Williams also assured the group that the Department of

---

[2] Guidelines which have been sent to the states to aid them in setting standards.

[3] The Clean Rivers Restoration Bill submitted to, and subsequently passed by, the Congress in 1966. This Act greatly expands aid to the cities by wiping out dollar ceilings on federal grants. Thus New York, which has been averaging only 1.1% in federal money for water pollution control, could now get between 30% and 55%. In aggregate, federal outlays for water pollution control are estimated to jump from $150 million in F.Y. 1967 to $1.25 billion in F.Y. 1971.

Health, Education, and Welfare had no intention of suggesting a single standard. This point was made clearly in Mr. Williams' response to a question:

BUSINESSMAN: We run smelters which emit all kinds of gases. When we have a smelter in the middle of New Jersey we spend fortunes to clean it up. Is it necessary to clean it up when we have one in some remote area of Montana?

PROF. AUSTIN:[4] This, I take it, is an air pollution problem?

BUSINESSMAN: Yes, air—SO_2. We take out all the SO_2 in the form of acid, which is readily recoverable and has some value. But in the middle of New Jersey—northern New Jersey—we spend a fortune to do it. We turn out air cleaner than the stuff we suck in.

MR. WILLIAMS: Well, by prevailing practice it is not generally expected that the smelter in the western state would be as well controlled. However, it depends on how closely you've looked at what adverse effects may come from it. If there are no farmers in the area who are suffering any crop damage, et cetera, you are probably all right.

The discussion continued with the following dialogue:

MR. QUIGLEY: If we set the standards back in the days when Billy Penn sat under the tree with the Indians, I think we could have one set of standards on the Delaware and maintain them. But we're not acting then, we're acting now and these are the realities.

PROF. AUSTIN: Let me be sure of this. Is this the position of Secretary Udall and Secretary Gardner—that federal standards would vary?

MR. WILLIAMS: With regard to air pollution, Mr. Gardner does not yet have the power to set standards.

PROF. AUSTIN: I understand that.

MR. WILLIAMS: All right. This gentleman is talking about air pollution emissions with regard to air pollution effects. Insofar as a smelter in an already polluted area, so to speak, would have an additive or synergistic effect on things, it would be expected to be more tightly controlled than one that was in some remote area.

MR. QUIGLEY: Tom [Williams], you've got to come out that way. You've already done that in your automobile standards. You have

---

[4] Professor Robert Austin of the Harvard Business School, who was acting as moderator of the discussion.

a different set of standards for a Volkswagen than you do for a Cadillac.

THE ESTABLISHMENT AND ENFORCEMENT OF STANDARDS

In the early phases of the discussion there was a noticeable difference of opinion as to who should establish and enforce standards. The government representatives all favored federal establishment of standards with as much local management of these standards as possible. Secretary Udall took this position in his opening remarks, likening pollution control to law enforcement. Commissioner Quigley reinforced the Secretary's position:

> I agree with Secretary Udall that there is a need for national standards. If Senator Muskie were here, I'm sure he would agree, in spades doubled and redoubled, because the idea of setting standards basically started with Senator Muskie. He was the originator of this approach.

Commissioner Quigley then outlined the procedure specified in the Water Quality Act of 1965:

> Keep in mind that the Water Quality Act of 1965, as it was finally worked through the Congress, gives the states, in effect, the first turn at bat in this game. The governors have a year—in other words, through October of this year—to indicate to the Secretary their intent to set the standards. The states do not have to set these standards. They could fail to do anything. They could just pass it up.
>
> If they indicate their intent by October 2—that they plan to set standards on the interstate waters that flow within their state or that form part of its coastal waters—they then have until July 1 of 1967 to come in with standards, or proposed standards. These standards are then to be reviewed by the Secretary. If they are found adequate and satisfactory, they in effect become the federal standards. Thereafter any deviation or violation of these standards in a stream could trigger the federal enforcement authority.

Mr. Williams likewise advocated nationally established standards, indicating that air standards were slower in developing than water standards.

MR. WILLIAMS: The automobile emission standards, which are the only federal standards available so far in the field of air pollution, are pretty much the same as those which are going into effect in California this fall and which will go into effect nationally for new cars, whether imported or made here, in the fall of '67 for the '68 model year. They will reduce the emissions of hydrocarbons and carbon monoxide by about 60%. This reduces these two constituents of car exhaust as far as is technically feasible at this time. The reason for reducing hydrocarbons is that this is the component which, along with oxides of nitrogen, produces photochemical smog, which is bothersome in all regions of the country. Carbon monoxide, as you know, is undesirable because it is a lethal gas if it reaches sufficiently high concentration.

PROF. AUSTIN: I take it that when and if you had the authority given you to clean up exhausts from power plants, for example, you would have the same kind of a standard: reduce the chemical content to such and such a figure.

MR. WILLIAMS: Yes. We don't have anything of that sort now. We are asked by Congress to establish codes of good practice which some people might consider the infant form of adult standards. Actually, what these amount to are attempts, at least for major industries, to determine what are the best available means today of operating different kinds of plants and of controlling them to the extent which is economically and technically feasible at this time. These we're developing with regard to major types of industrial installations.

In addition, we have been asked to establish air quality criteria, which do not have the same legal sanction as standards. These have to do with ambient air. We've been asked to establish standards for major air pollutants—not standards, but criteria. For example, on sulfur dioxide we're in effect saying: Here's what happens if a given level of sulfur dioxide is found in the ambient air; here's what happens to plants; here's what we think happens to people; here's what happens to various kinds of materials. When these have been published, they will, of course, be available for state or local control agencies to use if they want to establish standards. We have no authority to do so.

In contrast, the businessmen began by strongly advocating locally established and enforced standards, and pressed for details about how the federal government planned to encourage local participation:

I don't know how much I express the opinions of others, but I think we can all visualize a tremendous bureaucracy if water pollution enforcement is brought in at the federal level. The state and/or local level, as the case may be, would seem to be the more appropriate level to accomplish this.

I'm sure I may not be speaking for the total group in this respect, but I personally feel that there is much to be done in the area of pollution control, and business must make a substantial contribution to improve things. But I think the businessman would be far happier and far more comfortable with local and state standards and enforcement—and I'm thinking of real enforcement—than with the tremendous bureaucracy which could develop out of federal standards and federal enforcement.

Now, in order to bring about this objective, if it is valid, it seems to me that the federal government might consider a program where there is some incentive for the states and/or municipalities or other governmental agencies at the local level to make some progress in this area.

Commissioner Quigley responded:

Let me go back. The original water pollution control program, which went on the books in '56, and the Clean Air Act in '63 both provide for federal grants to state and, in the case of the Air Pollution Act, local agencies for the purpose of setting up or expanding existing state or local pollution control programs. This has not been a large program. The grants that have been made under the water pollution program have averaged $5 million a year, which, divided among 50 states, does not add up to tremendous sums. But the Delaware River Basin Commission receives a grant from us each year. ORSANCO[5] receives a grant from us each year. All of the state water pollution administration units receive a grant from us each year.

Now, in both the Muskie Bill and the Administration's Bill, it's proposed that this amount be doubled to $10 million per year. When I testified, I made a specific recommendation that this money be passed and made available in fiscal 1967, and that the new $5

---

[5] Ohio River Valley Water Sanitation Commission.

million be earmarked for the states to enable them to go about the task of setting the standards. Recognizing that most of these states are already under the gun—their legislatures have met and their budgets are fixed—it is going to be a real challenge for them to come up with the talent to do a conscientious job of setting standards. So our thought was that if the Congress would pass the pending legislation, which would make the funds available for '66, we'd go in on a supplemental request and make these funds available immediately to the states to help them do the job—those states which want to do it—of setting the standards.

In a similar vein, Mr. Williams assured the participants that one of the objects of HEW was to encourage communities to take action:

I think there has been a lot of emphasis, beyond what is perhaps necessary, on what the federal government is going to do, in a direct sense, to control air and water pollution. The setting of standards is very important. However, speaking for the air pollution program, the whole thrust of the Clean Air Act is to make it possible that air pollution be controlled at the state and local levels of government. Almost all the powers we were given are for that purpose, with the exception, perhaps, of the interstate abatement action. That was given because there are many cases in which the public has no recourse under law from pollution that is endangering their health and welfare from another state—no direct recourse.

The framers of the Clean Air Act recognize the importance of regional programs. They know good and well that you can't hold the air over Greenwich and not let it flow over New York or vice versa. So they tried to respond to that to some extent by offering $3.00 of federal money for every $1.00 of local money if two or more communities get together and establish an air pollution control district. Likewise, if a county embodying several communities will establish an air pollution control agency, it gets more federal support than the two-for-one federal support that goes to an ordinary agency.

The purpose of developing the criteria is to give local and state officials some guidelines to work with. Our whole research effort is devoted to giving information to industry and local and state governments to help them deal with the problem. We spend about

$3 million of our budget for technical assistance. This means that the local air pollution control officer can get in touch with the state agency or with us directly, and we'll send an engineer or some sampling equipment out there to help him appraise his air pollution problem. So let's not forget that the primary thrust of all of this legislation is not to do away with the local option or the sovereignty of states, but to help them to make it work.

As the discussion progressed, however, there were indications that some federal officials are somewhat skeptical of many states' willingness and/or ability to do the job. This was revealed in a dialogue between Commissioner Quigley and a businessman who was questioning the feasibility, much less the reasonableness, of the timetable set up by the 1965 Water Quality Act:

BUSINESSMAN: One gets a great deal of static from a lot of sources —mainly technical—that we do not know enough about what a reasonable standard is. Is setting standards within one year— standards on which regulation, investment and industrial practices are to be based—is that a practical proposition given the absence of biological and a whole lot of other knowledge which we haven't got today?

MR. QUIGLEY: I don't know whether it is practical or not. It is an assignment we have, and we are going to do the best we can to carry it out, and if we fail to do it, Senator Muskie and company will give us what for.

BUSINESSMAN: It's not you that are doing it. Well, in part it is. But if the governors of the states are to do it, with what technical knowledge?

MR. QUIGLEY: Well, of course, the answer that I think Senator Muskie would give to that if he were here would be that as far as he was concerned, the states never should have been involved in this. His initial proposal, as it was originally introduced, was for the federal government to set standards. The House amended the bill to provide for the states to set standards and the ultimate compromise that was worked out in conference was that the states would be given the first opportunity to set the standards. If they failed to do it, then the federal government would do it. So I think his answer would probably be to agree with you that the states can't do it and he never thought they could.

BUSINESSMAN: And therefore you can.

MR. QUIGLEY: No, therefore we must.

BUSINESSMAN: But you are also assuming that you can, and you just admitted that you can't.

MR. QUIGLEY: The Congress has given us this assignment and has given us, frankly, far more money than any state water pollution agency has. Now, I believe some of the states cannot do it. I think that some of the states not only can, but will.

. . . . .

The irony, of course, of the whole political process is that if this bill had remained in its original form and the responsibility for setting water quality standards had remained with the federal government, I am absolutely confident that we would never have set July 1, 1967, as the date by which we would have the job done. We would have gone about it in a much better organized, and a much more scientific, and a much more deliberate way. We would have caught hell from the conservationists for dragging our feet, but I think we would have programmed this thing out.

But, in the conflict between having the federal government do it all or keep it out completely, we came up with this inevitable compromise which says: all right, let the states do it; let's see what they can do in a year and a half. I frankly think some of them are going to surprise us by the good job they do. I think others are going to fall flat on their faces. I think others aren't even going to try.

Then, I think, we have to take what they do, and if we can approve it—fine. If we can't, we must go about the job of doing it on the basis of our present knowledge, recognizing that we are definitely going to set some standards too low and some too high. The test of the standard-setting process is going to be in its application; the only way we'll find out is to try.

By the end of the discussion, it had become apparent to a great majority of the participants that the states would probably default to the federal government in the establishment of standards, and that the timetable set up in the 1965 Act was designed primarily to put pressure on the states, not the businessman, at least during the first round.

Once the business participants understood: (1) that pollution standards would probably be federal standards, but (2) that they would be flexible in the sense of taking local problems into account, and (3) that the federal government intended to encourage local enforcement, most of them seemed quite willing to go along with the federal program. With one exception, they all agreed with Professor Austin:

> If you now understand that any federal standards that are set will vary with the conditions in the area to which they are applicable, would you agree that industry would be better protected by such flexible standards, managed by local groups, than if the standards were set helter skelter by state and municipalities absolutely freely?

WHO SHOULD PAY

Agreement as to who should establish and who should enforce standards in no way implied agreement as to who should pay to see that the standards were met. There was disagreement among businessmen as well as between business and government. One businessman felt quite strongly that pollution was a local problem which had to be solved at the local level at the expense of the polluters:

> It seems to me that the issue is very clear. The [background] paper points out that if everybody pollutes a little, and as more and more people do it, eventually you're going to have a pollution problem. Therefore, each person is responsible for what he does, he has got to pay for it, and it becomes part of the cost of doing business. I don't see that the federal government or the state government or anybody else except the people that are causing this pollution know enough about it to stop it. If you go on the assumption that industries have got to put the air back the way they found it, and if you assume the same for water, then there is no problem. Industry bears the cost and it's just specious reasoning and another in another state, that he doesn't have to do this. He's simply got to put the water back the way it was, and that means to say that because one guy lives in one state under one condition, the same purity, the same PH content and the same temperature.

Another agreed with Secretary Udall that the pollution problem has developed as a result of the urbanization which took place after most plants were built, and that the sudden imposition of standards discriminates unfairly:

The thing that would bother me about the approach of having steel mills in different places solve their problems on a local basis is that the plants were put there and the locations were chosen without pollution problems as a consideration. Now, we have these problems and the burdens are definitely unequal for reasons that have nothing to do with the requirements at the time of location.

Working under the assumption that pollution control is serving a social purpose, and that the government should assist polluters, attention then focused on the mechanism by which this could be done. Secretary Udall claimed that pollution control was a natural case for tax incentives. Later in the discussion, Professor Austin pointed out, in a discussion with Messrs. Quigley and Williams, that there was a fundamental difference between air and water, and, as Mr. Quigley pointed out, that air pollution control is probably better suited to a tax incentive than water pollution control.

PROF. AUSTIN: It seems to me that there is a fundamental difference between the water problem and the air problem and I'd like to get your reactions.

The air problem seems to me to be one where the standards which will come out—whoever sets them, whether it be the federal government or a state government or a municipal government—will have a direct impact on industry qua industry. The cost of removing the pollution from the air will be an industry job. The municipal job will be to set the standards and the industry job will be to live up to the standards.

If that is the fact, it seems to me there are fewer questions involved in terms of business leadership in air than in water, and there are fewer questions in terms of how you get a cooperative venture going. Industry will have the standard imposed, it will live up to the standard, it will pass the expense of living up to the standard on to the consumer, and there it is. Would you agree with that?

MR. WILLIAMS: I think that is true. I don't know whether it's that clear-cut, and Mr. Quigley may not agree. But I think it is true that with regard to the air pollution control problem, there is nothing comparable to the public monies that must be spent for sewage treatment plants, for example, in water. There is nothing comparable to that unless you want to include—which may be included one day—the problems of municipal waste disposal, much of which is by incineration. That may some day be a problem somewhat similar to the sewage disposal plants, but I doubt that it would reach the same magnitude.

PROF. AUSTIN: With water, on the other hand, you've got industries polluting water, you've got municipalities polluting water, and yesterday's *Christian Science Monitor* cites Senator Tydings as suggesting that the simple flushing of toilets out of boats is something that must be controlled, which is individual consumers as contrasted with industry. So, it seems to me that the problem of regulation and cooperation is a greater one. The problem of whether or not, for example, you give a tax abatement under the Federal Corporation Income Tax Law for investment in pollution control equipment is more applicable, as a discussion subject, to the water pollution problem than the air pollution problem.

MR. QUIGLEY: I agree with everything you say except the latter part. I would think the tax abatement concept would be equally valid and maybe, in some respects, more valid for air pollution than it would be for water. Water being what it is, there are industries that can and do hook on to a municipal system and thereby go a long way toward solving the problem. Air being what it is, you're not going to be able to channel it into the municipal system and let them clean it up and dispose of it. You're going to have to meet your problem at the top of your smoke stack and you're going to have to meet the whole outlay for it without any grants from the federal government directly or indirectly. So, I think if there is validity, and I think there is, to the concept of tax write-off, to me it would be as applicable to air pollution devices as it would be to water pollution control.

Expanding on the possibilities for sharing the cost of water pollution control, Commissioner Quigley outlined the current and potential future programs which provide for grants by the federal government to state and local governments for sewage plants that can then be used by businesses:

The present law has a grant construction program in it under which the federal government makes available to the states money which the states allocate to municipalities to assist the municipalities in the construction of sewage treatment facilities. The present program allows 30% of the appropriate approvable cost of the project or $1.2 million, whichever is less.

I think the Federal Water Pollution Program, as operated in the last ten years, has tended to be eminently successful in the larger towns and the smaller cities. This has been a very attractive program in the town of 25,000 or a city with 60,000. It has had little or no impact in our larger, major cities. We must recognize that these larger cities are the major source of pollution—that it does little good to clean up all the little towns up the river if, when you get down into the big urban area, there is gross pollution. You're only kidding yourself if you think that you are really cleaning up that river. A lot of sewage treatment plants may be built, and this might be good. But you're not really cleaning up that river.

Now, it's in an attempt to get at this problem that I think Senator Muskie and the Administration have both submitted bills to the Congress of the United States. In essence, what the Administration has said is that we will lift that $1.2 million project ceiling and we will pay the full 30% on all projects if the city will get together with its sister cities, perhaps in sister states, and develop an organized, coordinated program for doing this project, and doing it right; for maintaining and operating it in the future; for anticipating its needs; in other words, for putting the thing on a sound, fiscal, programmed basis. Muskie has come along, however, and he has said, in effect: "Let's just lift the $1.2 million ceiling on each project and let's give everybody 30%."

This basically is the issue between the Administration and Muskie, I think, at this particular point in time. We say lift the ceiling only if the states and the municipalities will go to the trouble of doing this thing right. Let's not just hand out the federal dollar willy-nilly and hope that the plants will be built in the right place and that they will be operated thereafter. What we're saying is: before we start spending the kind of money that we're now talking about spending, let's make sure that this thing is a little better organized than it has been in the past. This basically is the issue between the Administration and Muskie at the moment. How it is going to be resolved, I don't know.[6]

[6] See footnote [3].

No consensus was reached among the business participants regarding the desirability either of tax incentives for private investment or of federal grants to build and operate municipal facilities. Furthermore, no mention was made of other possibilities which have been suggested from time to time, such as the effluent tax currently being used in the Ruhr Valley in Germany.

COURSES OF ACTION

With no agreement as to how to pay for pollution control, it is not surprising that the participants never got to the point of systematically suggesting and evaluating courses of action. There were, however, some illustrations of what businessmen have done.

Regarding air pollution, an effective, but not universally applicable, approach was described by a smelter-owner in Montana:

> We buy an area eight miles wide and seventeen miles long—to leeward. That's our pollution control. We keep sheep on there. And they love it.

A more urban-oriented approach was outlined by John Ryan of Pittsburgh:

> I talked enough about Pittsburgh this morning, but I'd like to suggest this: I think we've done it. This was a cooperative venture with industry on both water and air.
>
> On this point about the availability of technical people—if you're going to start to invent the wheel all over again, you really don't have enough money to do it. What we did in Pittsburgh was to set up basic technical committees. When the law was revised about six years ago—and I happened to have been chairman of the overall committee—we set up basic technical subcommittees for the railroads, for the steel companies, for the chemical industry, and so forth.
>
> We had on these committees representatives—and I'm talking now of the professional chemical engineering or metallurgical representation—and these people were instructed to approach this job as a professional effort. What that did was to magnify enormously the technical abilities that could be brought to bear on this problem. You had the county ordinance and the city ordi-

nance and they were enforced by a few people—a couple of engineers. By these subcommittees you could bring many people together, and I can assure that the industry people, when you got down to it, were not special pleaders. They were professional people with a professional problem and they were charged by their bosses to arrive at a set of regulations that would satisfy the community needs and not be horribly burdensome on industry. We did arrive at this. The standards were outlined, the bill was passed unanimously, and we've gone on.

The real question has been the time scale over which this was accomplished. In other words, if you have a utility plant that's going to be obsolete within five years, it is silly to apply an ordinance control to that plant today. You should apply it five years from now. The same thing is true of the processes in the steel industry. The people knew in Allegheny County when these were going to be obsolete. So there was a selected time scale with a final limit, maybe, of ten years. We tried to sit down and work this out. If Ed Wideline, the former head of the Mellon Institute, were here, he would say that from his experience—and he is one of the authorities in the country on air pollution, at least—you've got to get at the technical guts of this thing.

A plea was made for channeling the limited federal funds into a few demonstration programs to develop approaches and techniques which could be widely applied when more funding became available:

It seems to me that in this whole discussion we're addressing a huge problem. We're talking about the United States. The only way that we are going to figure out what the problem is and what can be done about it is to take a small area—one basin, or one city, or some political grouping—and do this job. Let's find out how we get cooperation and establish a pattern of success. Once we've done that, then you can go ahead with it. You cannot make sporadic attacks and nibble at it here and there.

I don't think that competence-wise you can get the staff to do this thing on a national basis. I think that the only way to do it is to say: we are going to take Fitchburg, or Greenwich, or whatever place, and we are going to do this job and find out how to do it. We've got to get business to cooperate; we've got to get the local politicians to cooperate. Let's do it in one place. Think how much more you could have done with that money [$5 million] by just spending it in one place and showing what can be done. You would have worked out a pattern. You would have defined a problem, ended the argument about it, and done it. If we just dilute our efforts, I think we are never going to get it done. I feel that somewhere we should take a stand and have a sample program. Would this be possible? Would it be feasible? Would you put your five million in one little spot and do it?

Commissioner Quigley suggested some political difficulties associated with such an approach:

I think we have to recognize the realities of life in a democratic society—the practical politics. If the five million that we are talking about were to be earmarked for Rhode Island or the Delaware River, it would get unanimous, bipartisan support from Senators Javits, Kennedy, Scott, Clark, Williams, Case, Boggs, and Williams. In other words, you would get eight votes for and 92 against.

We have a demonstration grant program, that was authorized last year, to do something, or try to do something, new and different and imaginative on the problem of pollution from combined sewers. In some places, sanitary sewage and storm water sewage are collected in the same system. This is characteristic of most of our older cities, particularly in the East. Congress has said: here is $20 million a year for the next four years. You go ahead and spend that. They won't let us put all of that $20 million into one town or one city. We've got to divide the pie up. There are limitations as to how much can go into any one project.

Thus there is recognition of the demonstration concept, but once you get into an ongoing program, you've got to support all state water pollution agencies. You've got to divide the money among all interstate agencies. You can't give it all to ORSANCO, for example, or to the Delaware River Basin Commission. You have got to give it to them all.

It is clear from Mr. Quigley's earlier remarks that the Department of the Interior feels the approach used by industry on the Delaware River Basin is a model which bears special consideration by other groups in other river basins.

During the course of the discussion, two potentially troublesome aspects of any systematic program for pollution control, be it for the Delaware River or for Pittsburgh, were mentioned: (1) inter-industry cooperation and (2) intergovernment cooperation. John Ryan suggested that the keys to Pittsburgh's success were the joint committees and the careful programming of investment so as to coincide with equipment replacement cycles.[7] It is not at all obvious that companies in other areas will wish to share technical competence or will be willing to agree to encumber their investment programs with a community agreement on pollution control equipment, particularly if they operate on a nationwide basis.

Looking at the intergovernment problem, one businessman/local official put his finger on a critical problem:

> I'm a member of a local governmental body. I'm a member of the Board of Estimate and Taxation of the Town of Greenwich. The area of the town of Greenwich is 60 square miles. There is a relatively small industrial concentration. We are surrounded by a number of other local jurisdictions. The local politicians talk about the people who throw effluvia onto our beaches and pollute our air and all these terrible things that happen to Greenwich, some of which are true, of course. We have the problem of getting together with other local governments, and I think that is a great and practical difficulty on the governmental level.

While the illustrations of businessmen taking action and facing the problems of cooperation were revealing, they hardly served as a substitute for a careful analysis of the businessman's role in keeping the air and water clean.

SUMMARY

In retrospect, the discussion served to establish three things quite clearly. First, business must become seriously involved in the pollution problem and the businessman must assume a leadership role, if only to protect his own interests. Second, there is no such thing as a single "standard" environment; any standards which are established by any government agency will vary from

---

[7] It is considerably cheaper to build control equipment into a new plant than to install it in an existing plant.

place to place, depending on existing circumstances. Third, given that federal standards would be variable, most businessmen, in the interest of fair competition, would prefer federal standards, and, in the interest of efficiency and realism, would prefer to have these standards managed locally. In effect, the business participants accepted the federal government's present approach, once that approach was understood.

Reaching this kind of agreement required a great part of the time available for discussion. It is not surprising, therefore, that the more specific aspects of pollution control—economic incentives and effective organization—were treated in less depth. Many possible payment schemes were brushed over lightly or neglected altogether. Similarly, the issues raised by Secretary Udall about how to organize and how to develop a logical program were never explored in detail. As a consequence, there is still a long way to go. The economics must be tied to the standards in order that realistic tradeoffs can be presented to decision makers and, ultimately, to voters and consumers. The advantages and disadvantages of the Delaware River Basin approach and the Pittsburgh approach must be analyzed carefully. To what extent are they effective, and to what extent are they exportable?

As a result of discussing standards and the government's role in setting them, a dialogue was begun between business and government. To the extent that this dialogue continues on into the more frustrating aspects of getting the job done, the discussion will have served a valuable end.

Selected Bibliography

Battan, Louis J. *Unclean Sky* (New York: Doubleday, paperback).

Gilpin, A. *Control of Air Pollution* (Washington: Butterworth, 1963).

Goldman, Marshall. *Controlling Pollution* (Englewood Cliffs, N.J.: Prentice-Hall, 1967).

Graham, Frank, Jr. *Disaster by Default: Politics and Water Pollution* (Philadelphia: Lippincott, 1966).

Hanks, J. J. and D. H. Kube. "Industry Action to Combat Pollution," *Harvard Business Review* (September-October 1966, pp. 49-62).

Kneese, Allen V. *Economics of Regional Water Quality Management* (Baltimore: Johns Hopkins, 1961).

Litwin, J. *Control of River Pollution by Industry* (Chicago: Public Administration Service, 1965).

Mantell, H. N. *Industrial Incentives for Water Pollution Abatement* (New York: Inst. of Public Administration, 1965).

Stern, A. C. *Air Pollution* (New York: Academic Press, 1962).

CHAPTER IX

Conclusions

This conference covered an extremely wide range of topics and issues. There were three themes which permeated all the talks and discussions, however, and it seems appropriate to draw the conference together around these themes. First, there was a general feeling that the cities, while beset by many difficult problems, were not, by and large, in a state of crisis. Second, there was an awareness that the federal government has become increasingly active at the local level in recent years, and that this will have a significant effect on the business-government relationship in the cities. Third, there was a varying degree of uncertainty regarding the nature and extent of the businessman's involvement in the solution of urban problems.

The Crisis

To a certain extent, the May 20th Conference was convened because national attention had been drawn to the "crisis in our cities." Much of this attention was precipitated by a few local crises which occurred in rapid sequence—the Watts riots, the New York transit strike, the water pollution crisis in Lake Erie, the air pollution crises in New York and Los Angeles, et cetera.

Even a casual reading of the conference transcript, however, indicates that few, if any, cities are standing at the brink of disaster. Rapid advances are being made in housing technology, and, as the cities spread, a greater percentage of the population is living in acceptable housing. Baltimore appeared to be the only city where it was felt that something drastic had to be done about urban transportation. Pollution, while becoming more serious as a natural consequence of increased urban density, has hardly reached the point of poisoning our atmosphere and our water resources beyond recall. The quality of education, while not uniform, is rather outstanding in comparison with the education provided in most parts of the world.

This leads us to the conclusion that it is not a significant increase in the seriousness of the problems of the cities which has led to the cry of crisis. All indications are that these problems have been with cities for centuries, and that, if anything, things are getting better. What does seem to be happening is that the mechanisms for becoming aware of problems, and for contrasting existing conditions with ideals, are improving rapidly. This suggests that our response was not to the increased seriousness of the problems, but to our increased awareness and intolerance of them.

The Federal Role

It was no accident that the HBSA conference was held in Washington, and that the White House was involved. There were several indications that the federal government's view of its role in solving urban problems is undergoing rapid change.

The Demonstration Cities Act of 1966 gives the federal government a strong carrot to use in its efforts to blend social and physical planning. The federal coordinator adds a stick, should the carrot prove to be inadequate.

The Elementary and Secondary Education Act of 1965 gives the federal government a potentially powerful control over the critical 10% of each school system's budget which is devoted to innovation.

The Urban Mass Transit Act of 1964, and more recently the Urban Mass Transit Act of 1966, permit the federal government to make capital grants for mass transit, thus complementing its extensive Interstate Highway Program.

In August 1964, the Office of Economic Opportunity was formally assigned the task of fighting poverty, and in July 1965 the President's Commission on Law Enforcement and Administration of Justice was charged with inquiring into the causes of crime. Both groups are deeply concerned with the social aspects of urban living.

The Clean Air Act of 1963, the Water Quality Act of 1965, and the Clean Rivers Act of 1966 put the federal government right in the middle of the controversy over controlling pollution, and give it the resources and the authority to make its proximity felt.

This great burst of federal activity within the last three years has culminated in the formation of the U.S. Department of Housing & Urban Development under Robert C. Weaver.

Perhaps the most profound effect of these developments is that the federal government is, or soon will be, in a position to set the standards by which cities will be judged and rewarded in the future. While this is most apparent in the pollution field, where standards are spoken of openly, it does not take much imagination to see the qualification criteria for the Demonstration Cities Act, or the Elementary and Secondary Education Act, or the Urban Mass Transit Act turning into standards in the not-too-distant future. This is the "direct thrust" of which Mr. Robert Ryan spoke so eloquently.

The setting of federal standards raises two important questions. The first, and the most heavily debated question, is: How are federal standards to be mated with local economics? In the discussion on pollution, assurance was given that standards would vary from region to region. But some doubt remained as to the validity of setting any standards without a detailed analysis of the costs and benefits over time. The difficulty of making such analyses gets worse, of course, as the costs and the benefits become more difficult to measure.

The second question is a political one. The geographic areas for which the federal government wishes to set standards are not governed by one body. Frequently these areas encompass more than one state, and inevitably they include a large number of autonomously governed townships. The question is: How will the process of local government be affected by the federal government's focus on broad regions? If the discussions on pollution and transportation are any indication of things to come, the most likely effect will be the emergence of regional agencies, such as the Bay Area Rapid Transit District and the Delaware River Basin Commission, to handle specific problems. Extrapolating this trend, we might expect to find special district governments gradually taking over the functions of the local city governments. There are some indications that this is already happening in Los Angeles. This trend should provide the businessman with an opportunity to get in on the ground floor of a new form of government, and hence raises anew some questions about the businessman's role in his urban area.

The Businessman's Role

If the discussion groups were to be ranked in order of their ability to reach conclusions, they would fall as follows:

(1) Housing and Urban Renewal
(2) Pollution
(3) Transportation
(4) Education
(5) Social Problems

Bearing in mind the limitations of small sample size, this ranked list varies along some interesting dimensions. For example, the degree to which the problem area has historically been considered within the jurisdiction of local governments varies from low to high. Also, the degree to which the problem is a physical problem vs. a human problem and the ease with which the problem can be quantified and measured vary from high to low. This suggests that the businessman is more at home thinking about some kinds of urban problems than about others. He feels more comfortable with those which: (1) require a minimum of political involvement; (2) involve physical rather than human changes; and (3) can be quantified and measured.

Given these variations, what is the businessman's "responsibility" to his community? Some would argue that it is not surprising that the businessman finds some problems easier than others because of his training and experience, and that it is his responsibility not to meddle in areas which are primarily of a social nature and which are regulated by the democratic process. On the other extreme, of course, there are always those who will criticize the businessman for his lack of "community responsibility" and his unwillingness to become more actively involved in all aspects of urban decision making.

Neither group addresses the problem of business involvement squarely. The discussions suggest not that the businessman is more "responsible" for some problems than others, but merely that he is more familiar with some than others. Given the close and complex interrelationships between problems, there is clearly a danger in solving the familiar problem without appreciating its effect on the unfamiliar. The early experience with urban renewal comes immediately to mind. Shortsightedness in the establishment of policies for transportation, education, and pollution control are equally apparent.

The lesson, then, is not that the businessman does or does not have a "responsibility" to become active in his community. The lesson is that, before he does anything, he has a responsibility to know what he is doing. The city is a very intricate, complex blend of physical and human elements. Anyone who wishes to assume leadership in a city, be he a businessman or a local politician or a federal coordinator, must be willing to come to grips with this complexity before he can be deemed "responsible."

The conference provided ample evidence that, once informed, the businessman can be quite effective in the urban arena. Numerous instances of individual action were cited. There were a few examples—Pittsburgh's Allegheny Conference being the most notable—where businessmen collectively have served as the primary motivating force behind the successful revival of a city.

We must conclude, therefore, that the businessman has a big stake in the future of our urban areas, that he is perhaps more familiar with some urban problems than others, but finally, and most importantly, that he seems as well qualified as any to seek their solution. If valid, this conclusion has far-reaching consequences indeed. For it suggests that the legitimate concern of the businessman extends well beyond the problems of his own organization and encompasses, at a minimum, the health and well-being of those geographical areas which are soon to contain three-quarters of the nation's population. The businessman can no longer afford merely to respond to urban conditions. He must mold them, and he must learn to mold them well. As Mayor Cavanagh put it:

If not you, who?

If not now, when?

Participants in the HBSA Washington Conference

Robert N. Anthony
Assistant Secretary of Defense
Washington, D. C.

Robert W. Austin
Professor
Harvard Business School

George P. Baker
Dean
Harvard Business School

Robert D. Beals
Vice President
American Express Company
New York, New York

Jules Beuret
Director of Marketing
Automatic Retailers of America
Slater School & Colleges Division
Philadelphia, Pennsylvania

Thomas N. Billings
Controller
Copley Newspapers
LaJolla, California

David L. Birch
Assistant Professor
Harvard Business School

Charles Blaschke
Office of the Assistant Secretary
   of Defense for Manpower
Washington, D. C.

Donald R. Booz
President
Donald R. Booz & Associates, Inc.
Chicago, Illinois

James R. Bradburn
Vice President
Electronic Data Processing
Radio Corporation of America
Camden, New Jersey

John Brademas
Representative, Indiana
Washington, D. C.

John M. Budd
President
Great Northern Railway
   Company
St. Paul, Minnesota

George Carracio
Midwest Regional Partner
Arthur Young & Company
Chicago, Illinois

Lisle C. Carter, Jr.
Assistant Secretary for
   Individual & Family Services
Department of Health,
   Education, and Welfare
Washington, D. C.

Walter P. Cartun
Vice President, General Manager
Westinghouse Air Brake
   Company
Wilmerding, Pennsylvania

Albert V. Casey
President
Times-Mirror Company
Los Angeles, California

Jerome P. Cavanagh
Mayor of Detroit

Robert S. Cell
American Security & Trust Co.
Washington, D. C.

Paul W. Cherington
Professor
Harvard Business School

John B. Clinton
Staff Assistant to the President
The White House

John C. Colman
Vice President & Director
Corporate Finance Division
A. G. Becker & Co., Inc.
Chicago, Illinois

Frank A. Colombo
Executive Vice President and
    General Manager
J. L. Hudson Company
Detroit, Michigan

Wilbur A. Cowett
Partner
Wertheim & Company
New York, New York

Hollister Cox
Vice President
Marine Midland Bank
New York, New York

Frank J. Croke
Manager, Educational Planning
IBM Corporation
Armonk, New York

Philip Davidowitz
Research Fellow
Harvard Business School

George DeMent
General Manager
Chicago Transit Authority
Chicago, Illinois

Leonard Duhl
Department of Housing &
    Urban Development
Washington, D. C.

James C. Falcon
The White House

Dan H. Fenn, Jr.
Vice Chairman, Tariff
    Commission
Washington, D.C.

Stephen H. Fuller
Associate Dean for External
    Affairs
Harvard Business School

E. N. Funkhouser
Executive Vice President
American Metal Climax
New York, New York

John Garrity
McKinsey & Company, Inc.
Washington, D. C.

Charles N. Gebhard
Associate Director of Alumni
    Programs
Harvard Business School

James P. Giles, Jr.
President
American Cement Corporation
Los Angeles, California

Charles Haar
Assistant Secretary
Department of Housing and
   Urban Development
Washington, D. C.

Neil E. Harlan
Vice President-Finance
Anderson Clayton & Company
Houston, Texas

Kenneth T. Howe
Treasurer
Jenney Manufacturing Company
Chestnut Hill, Massachusetts

William B. Hurd
Acting Assistant Administrator,
   Transportation
Department of Housing and
   Urban Development
Washington, D. C.

Donald C. Hyde
General Manager
Cleveland Transit System
Cleveland, Ohio

Kenneth N. Jolly
Vice President Corporate
   Relations
Campbell Soup Company
Camden, New Jersey

Joseph C. Kennedy
Vice President
Corporate Trust Division
Bankers Trust Company
New York, New York

Arthur W. Keylor
Associate Publisher & General
   Manager
Life Magazine
New York, New York

John M. Kinard
President
Pacific Western Industries, Inc.
Los Angeles, California

Harry W. Knight
Booz, Allen & Hamilton
New York, New York

John C. Kohl
American Transit Association
Washington, D. C.

Ralph F. Lewis
Partner in Charge
   of New York Office
Arthur Young & Company
New York, New York

Tom Lilley
Director
Export-Import Bank of
   Washington
Washington, D.C.

H. C. Lumb
Vice President & Director of
   Law & Corporate Relations
Republic Steel Corporation
Cleveland, Ohio

John W. Macy, Jr.
Chairman
Civil Service Commission
Washington, D.C.

Lawrence Marcus
Senior Vice President
Neiman-Marcus Company
Dallas, Texas

James Mauch
Bureau of Elementary &
   Secondary Education
Department of Health,
   Education, and Welfare
Washington, D.C.

John T. Mauro
Director of City Planning
Pittsburgh, Pennsylvania

L. F. McCollum
Chairman
Continental Oil Company
Houston, Texas

Clark E. McDonald
Managing Director
Hardwood Plywood
  Manufacturers Association
Arlington, Virginia

Joseph B. McGrath
Director
Urban America, Inc.
New York, New York

William H. McLean
Assistant to President
Stevens Institute of Technology
Hoboken, New Jersey

Michael Michaelis
Manager
Arthur D. Little, Incorporated
Washington, D. C.

Don Miller
Executive Vice President &
  Publisher
Call-Chronicle Newspapers
Allentown, Pennsylvania

Lawrence E. Mock
Vice President & Treasurer
Harbison-Walker Refractories
  Company
Pittsburgh, Pennsylvania

Robert W. Morey, Jr.
Brown Bros. Harriman &
  Company
New York, New York

Reynolds A. Morse
President
Injection Molders Supply
  Incorporated
Cleveland, Ohio

Peter P. Muirhead
Associate Commissioner for
  Higher Education
Department of Health,
  Education, and Welfare
Washington, D. C.

Charles D. Orth, III
Director of Alumni Programs
Harvard Business School

Jack Pearlstone
Executive Vice President
Joseph Meyerhoff Corporation
Baltimore, Maryland

Robert B. Pease
Executive Director
Urban Redevelopment Authority
Pittsburgh, Pennsylvania

Donald S. Perkins
President
Jewel Tea Company
Melrose Park, Illinois

Carl H. Pforzheimer, Jr.
General Partner
Carl H. Pforzheimer & Company
New York, New York

Frank J. Pizzitola
Vice President-Consumer
  Products
Celanese Corporation of America
New York, New York

Donald C. Platten
Senior Vice President
Chemical Bank New York Trust
  Company
New York, New York

James M. Quigley
Assistant Secretary of Health,
  Education, and Welfare
Washington, D. C.

Thomas C. Raymond
Professor
Harvard Business School

Randall Reed
Vice President of Finance
Atlantic Refining Company
Philadelphia, Pennsylvania

Charles B. Reeder
Senior Associate-Economist
E. I. DuPont Company
Wilmington, Delaware

John T. Ryan, Jr.
President
Mine Safety Appliances Company
Pittsburgh, Pennsylvania

Robert H. Ryan
President
Regional Industrial Development
  Corporation
Pittsburgh, Pennsylvania

Lewis M. Schneider
Assistant Professor
Harvard Business School

John Searles
Metropolitan Development
  Association
Syracuse, New York

John C. Secrest
Vice-President-Finance
American Motors Corporation
Detroit, Michigan

Gerald W. Siegel
Vice President
Washington Post Company
Washington, D. C.

Charles E. Sigety
Attorney
New York, New York

Eliot I. Snider
President
Massachusetts Lumber Company
Cambridge, Massachusetts

Roger P. Sonnabend
President & Director
Hotel Corp. of America
Boston, Massachusetts

Philip A. Sprague
President
The Hays Corporation
Michigan City, Indiana

Milton S. Stearns, Jr.
Vice President, Commercial
  Loan Department
Fidelity-Philadelphia Trust
  Company
Philadelphia, Pennsylvania

Robert D. Stillman
Partner
Payson & Trask
New York, New York

H. G. Symonds, Jr.
Senior Vice President
National Bank of Houston
Houston, Texas